Garbed in Green
Gay Witchcraft & The Male Mysteries

Casey Giovinco

Garbed in Green

LIBRARY OF CONGRESS CATALOGUING-IN-PUBLICATION DATA

Includes bibliographical references.

Copyright © 2018 Casey Giovinco

All rights reserved. No part of this book may be reproduced or transmitted in any form or by any means, electronic or mechanical, including photocopying or recording, or by any information storage and retrieval system, without permission in writing from the publisher.

ISBN: 978-0-9998719-1-1

On the Cover: Artwork by Stewart A.
Project Editors: Thorn Nightwind; Stewart A.; and Shawn M. Shadow ("Afolabi"), Olorisa (Oni-Yemaya) and Spiritist (a.k.a. anxiety-ridden, nut-job, editor-in-chief).

Casey Giovinco

DEDICATION

I dedicate this book to Thorn Nightwind and the God and Goddess who were kind enough and wise enough to make him my initiator, my mentor, and my friend. Thank you for all that you do. I love you!

ACKNOWLEDGMENTS

This book could not have been written without the work of so many wonderful people. Above that, though, the work that we do in Gala, which this book is designed to augment, could not have been done without the dedication and commitment of some really wonderful witches. I would like to take a moment and thank them briefly for their support.

As you will find out further on in this book, I would never have embarked on this Male Mystery journey in the first place if it were not for the gentle and loving guidance given to me by my mentor in Witchcraft, Thorn Nightwind. Beyond his initial encouragement, Thorn has consistently provided me with a plethora of resources whenever I have asked for help. In the beginning of my research, he held my hand and provided a shoulder to cry on. As Gala Witchcraft grew into the tradition that it is today, he helped me iron out rituals, write the tradition's Book of Shadows, and initiate the witches who have become like family to me. I could not have done any of this from developing Gala to writing this book without his help, so first and foremost, I would like to make sure that my eternal debt of gratitude to Thorn is acknowledged.

Second, I would like to thank Stewart A., whose artistic vision and attention to detail has kept me on track all these years (both as a witch and as a writer). His eye for what is truly sexy and incredibly powerful along the Gay man's path through the Male Mysteries never ceases to hold me in awe. It was his vision for this book's cover that made me recognize the full scope of what we were attempting to do here. When I saw it, I felt like *an author* for the first time.

Since Shawn M. Shadow has come into my life, he has challenged me to take a second look at opinions that I held to be above scrutiny, and my life is 1,000 times better today because of his influence. He has helped me be more moderate politically, which came in very useful during the writing of this book. He has helped me to understand my own philosophy more fully by constantly questioning my assumptions. I could not have written the Baudrillard chapter without his assistance. He also kept my over-use of the comma (an under-valued grammatical tool, if you ask me) in check. At times, I am sure that being my voice of reason certainly drove him crazy, hence his wonderfully comical title as this book's "anxiety-ridden, nut-job, editor-in-chief."

Finally, I would like to thank every initiate of Gala Witchcraft who came in between 2013 and today. To the first three initiates, who believed in me when they had no reason to, and who stuck by me through all the trial and error, this book could not have happened without their assistance and patience. I will never forget that debt, which I owe them. I owe a similar debt to the subsequent generations of Gala witches. They allowed me to use their spirituality in order to test my theories and work out the kinks within our magical system. Our magic is as potent as it is today because of your kindness. Thank you all for standing by me and helping me to bring this book to light.

CONTENTS

	Preface	i
	Introduction	vii
1	Gay History	1
2	Mysterious Mysteries	12
3	Male Mysteries	20
4	Phallic Fortress	28
5	The Magical Dynamo	41
6	Gay Mysteries	50
7	Gay Mythology	61
8	Magical Training	72
9	Dedication Ritual	93
10	Fire Festivals	102

PREFACE

My own fascination with the Male Mysteries started after my formal training as a witch was already finished. Prior to that, I was like many people new to witchcraft. I came to this path in order to get away from an overbearing Christian God, and I genuinely wanted no mention of God or a masculine deity of any sort within my own personal practice. My mentor did his level best to introduce me to the God—he certainly invoked the Horned One in ritual, and he encouraged me to connect with the masculine energies outside of ritual as well. Unfortunately, no matter how good his argument or how moving our coven rituals were for me spiritually, my personal baggage with men prevented me from being able to fully appreciate the masculine energies on any real or lasting level.

By that point in my life, I had survived quite a lot of abuse at the hands of men. Long before I knew what it meant to be Gay, I had been bullied in school by other boys because of my sexuality. The bullying turned physical in middle school, and my parents had to send me to a private school for my personal safety. In college, I was raped by a Gay man who took me home from the Gay bar after one of his friends slipped something into my drink. (Apparently it was his birthday, and I was the gift!) I don't remember the actual events of the rape. I only remember dealing with the aftermath of that encounter. Being fully aware of the physical pain that my body was in when I woke up, however, I can assure you that what he did to me was certainly not consensual by any stretch of the imagination. From that experience, I contracted gonorrhea, chlamydia, and syphilis. The doctors treated the gonorrhea and chlamydia immediately, but somehow the syphilis slipped everyone's attention. It wasn't until a severe rash broke out all down my back and in-between my fingers that we finally caught it. Needless-to-say, I had very good reasons to hate men, and, at the time, I really did hate them.

During my entire training in the priesthood, I had two memorable experiences with the God that I can recall. Only two! However, those two experiences were perhaps the most transformative experiences of my life.

The first experience happened just after my first degree initiation into Witchcraft. A few days after the ritual, I had the most vivid dream. It was so vivid, in fact, that I can still remember every detail of it all these years later.

I was in a cinderblock room. There were stairs along one wall, and the only lights in the whole place were fires lit in antique-looking iron braziers, which hung on the walls. I was kneeling on a dingy, old mattress on the floor, and my arms were outstretched, pulled in either direction by iron chains attached to the side walls—think quintessential German dungeon porn.

Suddenly, the most beautiful man I have ever seen in my entire life descended the stairs. He was exceedingly tall and beautifully muscular. His long blond hair fell just above his shoulders. He looked like the very image of a male model in his naked glory.

He said, "We're going to play a game," as he reached the bottom of the stairs and approached a table, which was behind me. "I am going to cut out both of your kidneys, and if you scream, I will let you die. If you refrain from screaming, however, I will put them back, and we'll have sex."

I remember feeling him cutting into my back to get at the first kidney, and then, all of a sudden, I felt myself floating above my body, watching the experience from a bird's eye perspective. Apparently, I did not scream in the dream, because this beautiful man and I were in the process of having sex when I woke up. The dream was so vivid that I had to do an unexpected load of laundry later that day.

When I told my mentor about this dream, he told me that it sounded like I had been initiated by the God directly. This type of experience didn't happen to everyone who went through one of our initiations, but it wasn't uncommon, either. He told me to look at it as a sign that our initiation "took." Later on, I found out that many shamanic cultures have similar experiences connected to their initiation rites.

More fascinating to me though was the typical interpretation of the kidneys. When someone dreams about kidneys, it can symbolize that they are having a problem in getting their needs satisfied or their wishes fulfilled. Considering the sexual nature of the dream and my own aversion to other men (especially Gay men) at the time, I felt pretty certain that the God was helping to heal me of my hatred of both sex and other Gay men. It took a while to get this far, and at the writing of this book, I am still not fully healed from the experiences I suffered at the hands of other Gay men. However, I have come a long way. It is only in hindsight, all these years later, that I can see the scope of that success.

The second experience happened just after my third degree. One morning, shortly after my third, I had another rather intense dream involving the Horned God. This second dream was nowhere near as intense as the first. Even though it happened more recently than the other dream, I don't remember the specific details now, looking back on it. What I do remember is that, at the time, it was potent enough to get my attention. Upon waking up, I took my cup of coffee out onto the back porch to enjoy the crisp morning air, as had become my custom during that time. All of a sudden, the biggest buck I have ever seen appeared in my neighbor's back yard. He stood in full view of me on my porch with his majestic 11-point crown, looking at me, "calling" to me. (At the time, I worshipped an antlered God, so this was especially profound.)

Since I lived in Durham, North Carolina at the time, this event was even more impressive than it otherwise would have been. It's not like I lived out in the mountains or in some deep, untamed wilderness where this type of encounter would be a regular occurrence. For me, this was as much a sign of something I needed to pay attention to as anything else I had experienced in Witchcraft up to that point.

I'm not sure exactly how long the exchange between me and this deer was, but it felt like hours. I had been contemplating calling my mentor that morning after the dream regardless, but the deer sealed the deal. After he bounded off into the trees, I ran inside and got the phone. I immediately began describing my dream and my experience with the deer. Our entire conversation boiled down to one simple question, and when I asked that question, it changed the course of my life forever. In fact, that question spawned this very book.

"Where is the gay aspect of the Horned God?"

There are countless tales in myth and legend of the Goddess having female lovers, and these tales are readily accepted by mainstream society as a valid part of the traditional canon. I'm specifically thinking of tales of Artemis or the Amazons of Greek fame, but there are others. While it's true that there is plenty of mythology surrounding Gay male gods (Zeus, Hercules, Achilles, Cu Chulainn, Shiva, Gilgamesh, and more), it's also true that our society refuses to embrace this aspect of the more traditional mythologies surrounding these gods.

When a movie about a hero (like Hercules or Achilles) comes out in theatres, he is routinely portrayed as straight, and his romantic entanglements with women (or, more often than not, a particular woman) are the central plot that directors unfailingly choose to focus on. Think about the 2004 film *Troy* starring Brad Pitt. Just by watching that movie alone, you would never know that Achilles had a love affair with a young man or that it was his love for that young man, Patroclus (played by Garrett Hedlund in the movie), which spawned the hero's involvement in the Trojan Wars.

If the *Epic of Gilgamesh* is addressed in any capacity whatsoever, his relationship with Enkidu is invariably glossed over as simply "friends," but, sadly, this is the fate of all gay archetypes, mythic gods, and heroes in general. Even in the twenty-first century, it is simply not generally acceptable for the hero to be a Gay man. Gay men can be the sidekick, the comic relief, or even the villain, but the role of hero or universal sex icon is off-limits for Gay men in any mainstream project.

With that said, despite the prevalence of Gay male mythology in the traditional canon (for those who are willing to dig to find it), Witchcraft has notoriously been deficient in recognizing the Horned God's homosexual aspects in any meaningful way. The closest we, as Gay men, can hope to come to seeing our own loving relationships mirrored in a divine template within any traditional occult religion is what, in my opinion, amounts to lip service.

The general Pagan public will concede that the Horned God is omnisexual, but, to date, we have not seen any actual mythic representations that would validate that claim within the Wheel of the Year or any of the other standard mythologies that span the various branches of the Art Magical. The traditional take on the Horned God's "omnisexuality" amounts to him enjoying sex wherever he can find it, and being rather indiscriminate about his encounters or partners.

This "omnisexuality" does not embrace a concept of what Plato or the Greeks might call *philia*, which we can find in the stories of Gilgamesh, Achilles, or Cu Chulainn. Beyond the lack of deep, abiding emotional connection with a male spirit that is his equal, the Horned God's omnisexual desires are not even represented in the traditional Wheel of the Year mythologies. His relationship is exclusively with the Goddess in this context.

Instead of seeing a divine homosexual relationship played out mythically before our eyes, we (Gay men) are supposed to content ourselves with throw-away comments at a public gathering about the omnisexuality of the Horned God—what might as well amount to the cosmic equivalent of a hookup. Personally, as a Gay male witch who has struggled with the prevalence of hookup culture within the Gay Community, I don't appreciate this being the only version of male union offered to us in reference to the Horned God.

Now, don't get me wrong. I'm not saying sex for the sake of sex is necessarily a bad thing. In fact, if we're honest with ourselves, the desire for sex without the other connections is natural. Sex is one of the base drives of human existence, and, as a base drive, it is necessarily complete and whole unto itself. However, sex for the sake of sex is just sex. It's not the be-all-end-all, and it should not be used to define the entirety of the Gay male experience. There's more to our intimacy and connection than that, just as there is more to the relationship between the God and Goddess represented in the Wheel of the Year than just the procreative drive. With that in mind, I felt that a more robust explanation of the Horned God's sexuality was in order.

After explaining all of this to my mentor (albeit with a little more fire and fervor than I am showing here), he "voluntold" me to take on the challenge of finding what I called "the Gay face of the Horned God" within Witchcraft. At first, I read. I read everything. I read traditional books on Witchcraft and Wicca, like *A Witches' Bible* by Janet and Stewart Farrar. I read everything I could get my hands on by Gerald Gardner. I read Raymond Buckland. Then I went to some of the less-standard books on Wicca and witchcraft, and I read those too. I read books on what has taken on the name *Traditional Witchcraft*, and I read books completely outside the Western Mystery Traditions that looked like they might shed some light on the topic.

Over and over again, I failed to find what I was looking for, so I turned to other resources. I read myth. I got my hands on *Cassell's Encyclopedia of Queer Myth, Symbol and Spirit*, and, suddenly, doors began to open. I read it cover-to-cover. Then I found James Neill's book *The Origins and Role of Same-Sex Relationships in Human Society*, and I used that book's bibliography like a personal reading list.

I was beginning to make some headway in my research, validating some of my opinions, disproving others, and applying the good stuff about Gay male history and mythology to what I had been taught in my coven. To my delight and surprise, my experiments worked. I began writing about my experiences on a blog, and Gay men from around the country began following my research.

One thing led to another, and I found myself offering long-distance training to a few select Gay men around the country. We began a group video chat every Sunday afternoon for roughly two hours, and, within a year, I initiated most of those students to the first degree. Together, we formed a new tradition of Witchcraft, specifically for Gay men who wanted to incorporate the Male Mysteries into their spiritual and magical practices. That tradition is now called *Gala Witchcraft*.

Gala Witchcraft is a coven-based, initiatory tradition, and we are currently looking for Gay and Bisexual male seekers who wish to explore the Male Mysteries with us. If you decide that my style of witchcraft in this book resonates with you, reach out to us. There is a contact page at the very end of this book.

While I am very proud of how quickly Gala Witchcraft has grown as a tradition and the work that we have done together to help heal Gay men and re-introduce the Male Mysteries as a central component of Witchcraft, I recognize that our group is not for everyone. No group is. Because of our focus on the Male Mysteries as they pertain to men who love men, we only accept Gay and Bisexual men who self-identify with the *male* gender for initiation into our covens. This necessarily leaves out quite a bit of the population who would benefit from a deeper study of the masculine polarity, which is one of the reasons that this book has come to exist.

I also genuinely understand that our path is not for every Gay or Bisexual man. Some men will choose to remain solitary, learning on their own and assimilating information in their own time. Others will have already found their home within more traditional, mixed-gender covens, which is truly wonderful. As far as I'm concerned, there are many ways to reach the truth. Do what's right for you.

Beyond trying to empower Gay and Bisexual men, this book is for anyone who wants to know more about how the Sacred Masculine can enrich his or her personal practice of witchcraft. Whether you're Gay, Bisexual, or Straight, whether you're male, female, gender fluid, gender non-binary, or Transgender, whether you're solitary, already in a coven, or you're still searching for your path, this book can help you connect with the Sacred Masculine in a self-affirming way that is body-positive, Gay-friendly, and genuinely informative for occult practitioners, regardless of the path that they choose to follow.

INTRODUCTION

What do you think of when you hear the words *Male Mysteries*?

Do you immediately think of misogynistic, deluded conspiracists who refuse to acknowledge their own male privilege, while looking for yet another way to simply exclude women? If not, perhaps you think of a group of men sitting around a campfire, passing around the talking stick, sharing their feelings.

How about when I say the words *Gay Witchcraft*?

Do your thoughts immediately turn to sex magic (either alone, with a partner, or in a group of men who love men)?

None of this could be further from the truth!

Let's start off by addressing the objection that men who participate in the Male Mysteries are misogynistic and trying to exclude and/or silence women. That is no more the case than it would be if that same logic were applied to women. Some misguided (and insecure) men who witness women gathering together to celebrate the Female Mysteries might think that these women are man-hating, "femi-Nazis" who want to (at best) castrate or (at worst) kill all the men. Both of these arguments are equally unfounded and based in fear.

Some men who choose to start or participate in any male-only groups may certainly do so for the wrong reasons, and I can concede that. However, the same can be said for some women who choose to segregate themselves—some, but certainly not all. The only socially responsible thing to do is to be vigilant and constantly check our biases when we choose to exclude anyone for any reason.

Women who desire to explore the Female Mysteries exclusively with other women do so for a variety of reasons. Perhaps, there is something that these women feel they gain from working without men present. Another possible reason could be that they feel as if they couldn't fully be themselves and openly talk about some essential step(s) along that particular path in the presence of the opposite sex. It's exactly the same for men who want to explore the Male Mysteries in male-only groups when those men are exploring this path for the right reasons.

As for the Male Mysteries being composed of groups that take men out into the wilderness to sit around a camp fire, passing around the talking stick and sharing their feelings, there is absolutely nothing innately *male* or *mysterious* about any of that. Women have feelings. In fact, society has used women's feelings to subjugate, institutionalize, and demean (even demonize) them throughout the entire history of patriarchy.

Hysteria was a mental disorder attributed exclusively to women. Its name can be traced back to ancient Greece. It meant "wandering womb." The very name for the condition excludes men, since uteruses were and are the exclusive domain of female bodies. It wasn't until as late as 1980 (with the publication of the DSM[1]-III) that modern psychology formally recognized the fact that men could suffer from hysteria as well.

Because of their perceived "emotional instability" and their lack of physical strength (compared against the average man), women were viewed to be "the weaker sex." In a more aggressive version of that same philosophy, women who were viewed to be "highly emotional" (or even remotely sexual) were viewed to have succumbed to sin, and they were tortured for that "weakness." At various points in history, treatment of hysterical women included periods of forced abstinence and/or forced sex (rape), forced masturbation, which they, oh so politely, called "pelvic massage" (also rape, for the record), high-pressure showers, and even fire.

Today, we still find ourselves demeaning women in relation to their emotions (sexual or otherwise). When a man's advances are spurned by a disinterested woman, he feels justified in calling her a "cold-hearted bitch!" If, on the other hand, a woman is too emotional, she's "dramatic," she's being a "drama queen," or she just likes to "make a scene." Her emotions are reduced to a trivial but uncomfortable entertainment. Even when no actual physical woman is present in a particular situation, we, as a society, demean men who are "too emotional" by taunting them with effeminacy (with being weak, "like a woman"). The *Collins English Dictionary* bluntly defines the word effeminate as "Having the qualities generally attributed to women, as weakness, timidity, delicacy, etc.; unmanly, not virile."

---

1 DSM is a common abbreviation for the Diagnostic and Statistical Manual of Mental Disorders, which psychologists and psychiatrists use to diagnose people when providing therapeutic treatment.

Nothing about embracing or expressing emotions has any gender identification whatsoever. Taking it out into the woods doesn't change that. Neither does adding a bonfire to the experience, nor does excluding women. Even the "phallic nature" of the talking stick fails to make this potentially therapeutic event into an intrinsically *male* experience.

When you look at the hallmarks of the Female Mysteries, you can see what I'm getting at here. The Female Mysteries talk about the menstrual cycle, childbirth, and the remarkable ability of women's bodies to nurture, feed, and sustain children. These are qualities that are exclusive to women, things that men simply cannot understand on more than an intellectual level, and since Witchcraft is a religion that keeps balance as one of its central tenets, it stands to reason that the hallmarks of the Male Mysteries (at least as far as they are explored along the witch's crooked path) would be equally exclusive to the male embodied experience. They would encompass things about being embodied in a male body that women simply cannot understand on more than an intellectual level.

As for Gay Witchcraft, perhaps the biggest misconception surrounding this topic is the idea that it is extremely sexualized. Unfortunately, this seems to be the fate of anything labeled *Gay*. However, there is nothing innately male (or Gay, for that matter) about sex, sex magic, or an orgy. These things have absolutely nothing to do with an exclusively Gay male tradition or style of Witchcraft.

Women masturbate. Women crave sex with a partner, and, just like some men, some women crave sex with multiple partners. If they are witches or magically-minded occultists on some other path, some women desire to learn how to put sex to good use in their own magical and spiritual practices, just like some (Gay) men do. For the record, there is absolutely nothing wrong with any of these activities, but, personally, I fail to see why most Gay men who pursue the concept of Gay Witchcraft as their spiritual path immediately do so by diving into orgiastic fantasies.

Sex is a human experience, plain and simple. It is not an exclusively male experience (Gay, Bisexual, Straight, or otherwise). Despite the peace, serenity, and wisdom that can be gained from fully-embracing one's sexual desires within the sacred context, sex, itself, reveals nothing about the (Gay) male embodied experience that it does not also reveal about any other embodied experience. Sex is a universal mystery that all witches embrace in one way or another, regardless of their physical sex organs, their gender identity, or their sexuality.

I only press this point because there is so much more to Gay men energetically, magically, and spiritually than the simple fact that we have sex with other men. Our ancestors understand the unique and special place that we held within their spiritual frameworks. Modern Gay men have lost sight of our ancestor's wisdom only because society has said that we are "unnatural."

It wasn't until 1973 that homosexuality was removed as an actual mental disorder. Now, that sounds like it was a "win" for Gay people, but, in truth, both the DSM-III and IV classified homosexuality in other unflattering ways. The DSM-III classified it as *ego-dystonic homosexuality*, which basically means that the person in question suffers from thoughts and behaviors that are in conflict with the needs and goals of a healthy sense of self. It's important to note that this was not meant to pertain to every case of homosexuality a therapist might encounter. Supposedly, it only pertained to cases where the patient was in distress regarding their homosexual desires, but the fact that it remained in the DSM at all was a strike against all homosexuality for many people. The DSM-IV talked about homosexuality as a *paraphilia*, which is a very clinical way of saying that someone's recurring sexual thoughts or fantasies are distressing to them, personally. It wasn't until the DSM-V that homosexuality was completely depathologized, and the DSM-V was only published in 2013!

More to the point, as homosexuality has left the DSM as a diagnosable condition, *"transsexualism"* (that's pulled directly from the DSM, by the way) got its turn in the spotlight. In the DSM-V, non-cisgender people are classified with the same political compromise of *dystonia*, which was placed on Gay people in the DSM-III. Today, Transgender people are classified as having *gender dysphoria* in the DSM-V. Though there are certainly differences between the Transgender and the Gay male experience, an attack on Transgender people still reflects negative feelings against Gay men and, ultimately, women. This is not a win for anyone.

This unfortunate bias within psychology (and within the society at large) stems from a very Christian-influenced and patriarchal misconception that homosexuality is "unnatural." One look at the animal kingdom will show you how patently false this notion is. Regardless of the evolutionary development of the species, homosexuality is prevalent everywhere.

Reptiles, birds, and even mammals exhibit homosexual behavior both in the wild and in captivity. In fact, what is most interesting, scientifically speaking, is that homosexuality is even more widespread among mammals than some of the lower order species. An argument might even be made that the more evolved a species is, the more abundant the cases of homosexuality will be whenever that species is studied. Scientists have reported extensive homosexuality activity in rats, mice, guinea pigs, bats, porcupines, raccoons, dogs, cats, hyenas, lions, elephants, horses, donkeys, cattle, porpoises, and whales, and in all of the various branches of the primate family tree.

Within the animal kingdom, homosexuality serves several functions. It relieves tension when heterosexual pairings are unavailable. It provides beta males (and females) with sexual release. It has been used as a survival strategy by smaller males who co-exist in prime territories with larger males. In some cases, mostly among mammals (and, specifically, among primates), homosexuality has been used to express genuine affection. In fact, there are even documented cases of exclusive homosexuality in lions, dolphins, and primates.

Many bigots would like to claim that despite the fact that animals engage in homosexual behavior, human beings are above that, which, again, is simply untrue. In fact, prior to Christianity and patriarchy taking root within Western Society, homosexuality was embraced as a fact and a natural part of life.

There is a scientific theory within the field of genetics, which seems to hold sway here. The theory states that if a behavior or quality persists through several generations, it must serve some evolutionary function. That homosexuality is a persistent trait within the human species can be seen by looking at the countless documented historical, anthropological, and sociological records regarding its practice consistently from ancient times through modernity.

While any guess at what that evolutionary function of homosexuality actually is would be purely conjecture at this point, some scholars have posited some rather interesting theories. Considering that we know that Gay men would often stay behind in the camps helping the women with domestic duties and rearing children, it's entirely possible that camps with Gay men in attendance would have been more secure than camps without Gay men present. The presence of a man in camp ready to fight when the warriors were off fighting or hunting may have saved the clan's next generation. While it's not even remotely scientific, mythology certainly backs that theory up. If nothing else, having Gay men around would have provided an extra pair of hands for the necessary work of gathering of food or the production of clothing or tools. The clans with Gay men would have been safer and more productive. Ultimately, what this amounts to is the simple fact that most people alive today could potentially owe their very existence to a Gay ancestor.

Our ancestors did not suffer from the disease of homophobia, which our current culture chronically endures. In fact, throughout history, exclusively Gay men and gender non-conforming individuals were prized as spiritual authorities and magical workers in nearly every culture you can name. The most common example of this is the Native American *Two Spirits*, but there are others. The counterpart to the Two Spirits in the South Pacific island cultures were called *mahus*. In Mesopotamian culture, there were numerous homosexual priestly casts. The Sumerians had a priestly cast whose involvement in homosexual activities was part and parcel of their priestly function. These *gala*[2] priests even took their name from the signs for *penis* and *anus* in their language. There are even mythological accounts of the gala priesthood engaging in homosexual activity. One Sumerian proverb reads "when the gala wiped off his ass, he said, 'I must not disturb that which belongs to the Goddess.'" When the gala priesthood engaged in an act of sacred sexuality where they embodied the Goddess, the man's ejaculate was viewed as a petition or gift to the Goddess.

Akkadian texts talk about the *kurgarru*, who were closely related with another priestly cast called the *assinnu*. The assinnu, like the gala priests, revealed the sexual function of their role through their name. The word *assinnu* has the same root word within their language as a word that means "to practice anal intercourse." Presumably, the assinnu priests were receptive during this anal intercourse, like their Sumerian counterparts. The Phoenician goddess Astarte was worshipped by the *kelev*, homosexual temple personnel. The Anatolian goddess, Cybele was worshipped by homosexual galli priests. As late

---

[2] The Gala Witchcraft tradition took its name from their Order as a point of remembrance and respect. Gala does not claim to be carrying on the same role, function, or style of worship in the same manner as the Sumerian gala priests. Gala Witchcraft does NOT claim to descend from that august order in an unbroken, ancient lineage. Instead, it takes their name simply as a way to remind its initiates and others that men who love men have a purpose within society.

as the seventh century B.C.E., the Hebrew faith had male homosexual temple attendants (the *kadesh*) for their goddess. In India, the Goddess was worshipped by transvestite devotees called *hirjas*, and her temple personnel included male and female cult prostitutes. This practice was going on well into the 20th century. Regardless of the culture, it seems that Gay men were meant to serve a spiritual function within the religion of the society in question.

Considering this exalted history, why would anyone willingly trivialize that incredible legacy by reducing its modern incarnation into yet another sex club? Most Gay men whom I talk to are greatly distressed by the shallow nature of the larger Gay Community. Even the Gay men who participate in club or bar culture and who seek sex on hookup apps only do so begrudgingly because there seems to be no other viable alternative available to them. So, I ask again: Why reduce Gay Witchcraft, the Male Mysteries, or one's spirituality (whatever it might be) to yet another version of an already broken system?

After people get over the fact that Gay Witchcraft is not going to be all orgies and sexcapades (though it can certainly include sacred sexuality, sex magic, and the like), the next misconception is that *Gay* and *Transgender* are the same and that they should be dealt with in the same way. I cannot tell you how many people ask me about initiating Transgender men when they find out that I do Gay Witchcraft or the Male Mysteries.

The reality is that it is not a simple answer, because people are not easily placed in boxes. While there is certainly overlap between the Gay male experience and the Transgender experience (both in the mundane realm and the spiritual), there are far too many places where these two paths diverge to effectively treat them as one and the same. While I, as a Gay man, have questioned my sexuality and played with my gender expression, I know nothing about what it is like to question the actual physical sex of my body or to suffer mentally, emotionally, or physically because that physical sex doesn't match up with my internal self. How could I lead someone else down that path to healing? Sex and gender are not the same thing, but neither are gender and sexuality.

If you're practicing Gay male Witchcraft, then you are necessarily practicing at the crossroads of the embodied male experience and the Gay experience of loving another man. Both need to be present to be effective. That means that, first and foremost, you must self-identify within the *male* gender. Although the Male Mysteries readily embrace and even require androgyny, the people who choose to participate in the Male Mysteries must still self-identify with being *male*. While there is nothing wrong with being gender-fluid or gender non-binary, it is necessarily outside the scope of what either of the Gendered Mysteries (Male or Female) are talking about. Conversely, if you are engaged in the Male Mysteries within a Gay Witchcraft tradition or style of magic, then your desire for other men is also a necessary prerequisite of initiation into that particular energetic current. Because the Male Mysteries practiced within the structure of Gay Witchcraft are designed to heal Gay men of the damage done to them by the overarching society and by each other, it is essential that they be practiced in homogenous groups with other men who love men.

Furthermore, Transgender people cannot be exclusively encompassed within only the Gay Community. They're reach is much larger. They are straight men and women. They are also Gay men and Lesbians. Some Transgender people continue to self-identify with the Transgender Community after they have effectively transitioned to their satisfaction. Others do not.

I genuinely believe that Transgender people have another essential Mystery to explore and bring to light for the world. The Male Mysteries alone do not fully encompass the depth or the breadth of the Transgender experience, and neither do the Female Mysteries.

Just because the Transgender Mysteries (if you want to call them that) don't fall under the Male Mystery umbrella or the Gay Witchcraft umbrella doesn't mean that they aren't valuable or necessary. They are! I have said this since I took my first Gay male witch into Gala Witchcraft, and I am putting it down here for the record:

I am patiently awaiting the day that a Transgender seeker wants to work with me to start a coven that explores the Mysteries associated with his/her/their particular path. I would love to help someone who is qualified bring those Mysteries to light.

That said, when talking about Gay Witchcraft, it is a very specific thing that we are talking about. It is not regular Witchcraft minus the women. Gay Witchcraft (as far as it pertains to men who love men) is only Gay Witchcraft when the Male Mysteries are attached to it. Otherwise, it's just witchcraft with Gay men in it.

1 GAY HISTORY

In an article published in the August 15, 2017 edition of The New York Times, Nathan Englander said, "While harking back to my pious, head-covered days, I am reminded of a notion that our rabbis taught us: The theft of time is a crime like any other. Back then it was about interrupting class—one minute wasted was a minute of learning lost. But multiply that minute by everyone in the room, and it became 15, 20 minutes, half an hour's worth of knowledge that none of us could ever get back."

In 1939, there were 16 million Jewish people in the world. As of 2016, there were only 14.41 million Jewish people. The Jewish population still has not recovered from the Holocaust. Just for a moment, take pause and imagine how many minutes of learning have been lost because of this gross hate crime, which the Nazis perpetrated on an entire group of people.

Englander was talking about life lessons, which he learned from the recent clashes in Charlottesville, but his recollection brings some temporal wisdom for Gay men as well. We, as Gay men, have had our very existence erased from the annals of history. We have had countless centuries stolen from us—not minutes, centuries! Like the Jews, we have been rounded up, persecuted, and killed. Lest we forget, Gay men (and women) were in the concentration camps alongside the Jews. In fact, that's the origin of the pink triangle as a connection to the Gay Community. The Rainbow Flag was created by Gilbert Baker to free us from that Nazi association and give us back a sense of pride. Therefore, it seems only fitting that a book meant to empower Gay men magically and spiritually should start with a brief history of Gay men in magic and spirituality. Time and time again, throughout history, Gay men have been held up as spiritual authorities and keepers of wisdom. It is only our modern homophobic and misogynistic culture that seeks to deny this prolific connection so vehemently.

"Garbed in green" was a phrase used in ancient Rome to indicate that a man slept exclusively with other men. They used it like we might say "fairy," "light in his loafers," "soft," or "sensitive." However, this particular seed, plucked directly from the Roman grapevine has born real fruit for the Gay Community throughout history. Oscar Wilde, with his green carnation, is perhaps the most famous example, but there are others. John F. Meagher put it plainly when talking about homosexuals: "Their favorite color is green." Barbara Gittings, the famous Philadelphia Lesbian activist, used to wear green in her youth to signal her own sexual orientation. It has even been suggested that James Joyce used the color green to hint at homosexuality in *The Dubliners*. The link between this color and homosexuality is subliminally pervasive within humanity's collective unconscious.

As Gay male witches, what better connection can we hope to secure for ourselves than a direct link back to Nature? *The Great Book of Magical Art, Hindu Magic and East Indian Occultism* says that "Green is the king of colors, probably for the reason that the Great Architect of the Universe chose it for the universal color, and that of Nature's primeval garment." Even our Wheel of the Year, a central component of the witch's spirituality, constantly reminds us that we should look to Nature for our answers. As I have said, our enemies shout that our existence is "unnatural!" How wonderful is it that their own prejudice undermines their baneful hate! How great is it that one of the oldest slurs used against us can be a uniting banner to help us fight against one of the newest?

One of my favorite things that my mentor in Witchcraft ever told me was to listen to my enemies. Our enemies do us a great service with their slurs and slander. By taking what ultimately amounts to a minor failing in our personalities and blowing it out of proportion, our enemies better enable us to address the issue before it becomes a real problem in our lives. Our friends, however, have a vested interest in keeping us happy, and they will often make excuses for our faults or cover them up from our vision completely. A clever witch learns to use his enemies effectively.

Gay men have no shortage of enemies today, so, to my mind, we are well-positioned to take advantage of this cunning advice. As many would-be Gay male witches have learned when attempting to join a traditional coven, Christians are not our only enemies in the religious sphere. Many old guard witches genuinely (and wrongly) believed that Gay men could not practice witchcraft. In fact, this particular debate has been going around since the very beginning of witchcraft's 20th century emergence from the broom closet.

While on one of her many tours of the United States, Sybil Leek was asked about the place of the homosexual in witchcraft. At first, this question stumped her something fierce. Never one to give up on a good fight, though, Sybil made a point of researching the topic and formulating an answer to that nagging question. In her book *The Complete Art of Witchcraft* (published in 1971, for the record), Sybil dedicated an entire chapter to the value of homosexuality in witchcraft. Ultimately, her conclusions informed a great deal of my own, and they served as a catalyst for much of this book. I highly recommend that you read that book.

Despite having evidence to the contrary, many people mistakenly lump Gay and Transgender people together. Sybil Leek did so in her book, but she was a product of her time, and did not have the abundance of information available to her that is available to us today. I am certain that if Sybil were still alive today, she would have written about Transgender people in witchcraft as well as Gay people.

While, admittedly, our histories share a lot in common, the historical accounts of Gay men and Transgender individuals are not spiritually identical. It is essential for the benefit of both groups that we recognize the historic energetic differences while preserving the all-too-necessary and appropriate political alliances, forged within the modern LGBTQIA Community.

I do my level best in this book (and specifically in this chapter) not to compound that mistake, to treat both groups with integrity and respect as separate (but allied) populations. When it is either impossible to separate the two histories or unclear what the sources say, I will be upfront about that. Information that is exclusive to the history of Transgender people has been left untouched for someone more qualified than me to discuss.

In that chapter, Sybil Leek made a connection between the homosexual "temperament" and religion, especially when discussing ecstatic or revelatory spiritual paths. Our ancestors seemed to have understood this wisdom intuitively. Whether you are talking about the most isolated tribe or the largest empire, this connection was honored in the ancient world.

Homosexuality is common, and its connection to shamanism is apparent in nearly every tribe residing near the Bearing Straits. Within several of those tribes, it was a common practice for young boys to adopt the roles and dress of women and apprentice themselves to an older shaman. More often than not, the apprenticeship had a sexual component to it. While this gender transition was viewed as immoral by the larger community, it was viewed as a sign of great power by the tribal shamans, who believed that the tribe's primary deity was, in fact, influencing the transition. Conversely, effeminate Gay men (as opposed to what we would identify today as Transgender women) were highly prized within the general community and regarded as magical.

While we have a tendency to think of the Native American *Two Spirit* concept as heavily connected to Transgender individuals, many of the tribes throughout the Americas acknowledge the existence and value of exclusively homosexual men under that umbrella as well. In South America, the religious leader or shaman was often a sexually ambiguous male, who took the receptive role during sex with other men. It is unclear what "sexually ambiguous" means in these references, because they could be referring to Transgender. The references could also be referring to what we might identify as *gender non-binary* or *gender fluid*. Two things, however, are abundantly clear. Regardless of how these shamanic figures self-identified, they were viewed to be of the male sex, and they took the receptive role with other male sexual partners.

Most of our modern accounts of these South American customs come from imperialistic missionaries, who recorded their derogatory opinions of what they were seeing among the native populations. Due to the negative slant that these records tend to have, I will not reproduce them here in full. Instead, I will merely generalize and acknowledge that buried beneath their bigotry are real accounts of actual customs, which native peoples held sacred.

"Transvestite" shamans seemed to be universal among the South American tribes and were reported in Chile, Argentina, Venezuela, Columbia, and Brazil. It is unclear whether the archaic term *transvestite* is meant to refer to what we, today, would refer to as *Transgender* or whether the accounts are simply referring to gender variant men. What is clear, however, is the value that these spiritual leaders had within their individual communities.

North American Two Spirits normally took on an androgynous appearance. James Neill tells us that the North American Two Spirit was often more androgynous than outright feminine. In some tribes, like the Navajo, there was no distinction between Two Spirit males and other males within the tribe, which leads me to hypothesize that, at least for the Navajo, the Two Spirits being discussed were exclusive homosexual men. The ability to balance both genders within themselves was certainly essential to the Two Spirit role, however, the outward expression of that balanced nature could happen anywhere along a spectrum.

Our modern conception of the Two Spirit role as being exclusively or primarily Transgender stems from the ignorance and prejudice of the European invaders who viewed the attire and manner of these individuals to be "too effeminate" to be considered respectably male. Since the Europeans didn't have a concept of a third gender, they had no appropriate language or frame of reference by which to filter their experiences with the native populations.

Not all Two Spirit individuals were Transgender. Some certainly were, but a great many of them were exclusively Gay men. Young boys who would become Two Spirits were usually identified early on by their interest in feminine things. They tended to play with young girls or to segregate themselves away from other boys. In our own society, this is still one of the tell-tale signs by which most adults presume a young boy may grow up Gay.

The North American tribes revered Two Spirit individuals as more spiritually elevated, which completely confounded the Europeans. Because of their spiritual (magical) gifts, great care would be given to the upbringing of Two Spirit children. As they grew into adulthood, these Two Spirit individuals would be shown great respect. Two Spirits were leaders of all the tribe's religious ceremonies, and tribal councils relied heavily upon their wisdom.

The European prejudice against "effeminate" men was unfounded at its base, and their inability to see the Two Spirits accurately revealed the depth of their prejudicial blindness. The drastic difference in cultural philosophy made it almost impossible for the European invaders to get a clear grasp on the actual function of these powerful people. While many Two Spirits often wore women's clothes and did "women's work," they were also viewed as strong and athletic by the Native populations who honored them. Had the European invaders bothered to look beyond their own insecurities while interacting with the native tribes, our own account of this majestic piece of Native American culture would be significantly different than it currently is today.

While a variety of individuals could fill the shamanic role for the

Native American tribes, the Two Spirit's inborn balance of polarity made them ideal for the task. In fact, a Two Spirit shaman was viewed to be exceptionally powerful. In instances where the shaman and the Two Spirit were separate individuals, the Two Spirit took precedence spiritually, socially, and politically.

Similar traditions existed within the island cultures of Polynesia. *Mahus* (the Two Spirit equivalent in that culture) were found from New Zealand to Hawaii. The word *mahu* means "to heal." In Samoan, a related word, *mafu* means both "to heal a wound" and "a male homosexual."

The Mahu role was not confined to healing, however. Like the Native American Two Spirits, the Mahus played a significant role in traditional religion. Mahus were ritual dancers who were revered. All the major chiefs throughout history have taken them as spouses. Let that sink in for a moment.

There seems to be a common misconception that Africa did not have homosexuality prior to the European invasions. This theory is malicious homophobia. The simple fact is that, contrary to African American machismo, there is widespread and voluminous evidence of homosexuality in Africa prior to encounters with European cultures. Wayne R. Dynes compiled and published a list of articles and monographs found in professional journals on various aspects of homosexuality among Sub-Saharan African peoples. I have included Dynes's *Ethnographic Studies of Homosexuality* in the bibliography of this book, in case you want to explore homosexuality in Africa beyond this book's scope.

Aside from being nearly universal in every facet of society, especially in adolescence, homosexuality played a significant role in the spirituality of African tribes. The *Mugawe* was a powerful cross-dressing, shaman-like figure, who served as a religious leader in Kenya. He was also a receptive homosexual male more often than not. In Angola, a similar spiritual figure serves as a diviner and healer. In Nigeria, there is a spirit possession cult that practices cross-dressing and receptive homosexuality. For the Zulu tribe, most diviners were women, but when a man did practice the art, he also engaged in cross-dressing and receptive homosexuality.

The link between homosexuality and spirituality does not exist exclusively within tribal cultures. Even the most advanced civilizations, dating back to the dawn of time, have embraced the spiritual gifts of

Gay men. Archeological remains from Mesopotamian cultures reveal the prevalence of homosexuality.

In fact, ancient Mesopotamia probably had more specifically Gay male priests than any other culture to date. Aside from serving as male temple prostitutes and courtiers, which were a legitimate subset of the priestly castes, the homosexual priests also conducted rituals and held official positions within that civilization's various hierarchies.

Third millennium Sumerian temple records refer to gala priests, who sang "heart-soothing laments" for the Goddess. The gala were not exclusive to Sumer; however, they are referenced within Babylonian and Assyrian texts as well. Akkadian texts talk about the kurgarru and the assinnu, which were complimentary priestly roles (discussed earlier in this book).

In fact, exclusively Gay male priests could be found in every variation of worship of the Great Mother Goddess within this culture. Even the early Israelites, who have ties to this region, included a goddess in their worship. The *kadesh*, whom I mentioned earlier (albeit briefly), were her male homosexual attendants, and they functioned within the temple compound in Jerusalem as late as the 7th century B.C.E.

While we are talking about the Hebrew faith, let's take a moment and address the popular argument leveled against us by those Christians who oppose homosexuality so vehemently. The sin of Sodom! Biblical scholars have noted a total absence of a prohibition against homosexuality in the pre-exile portion of the Old Testament. By all accounts, Lot's venture to Sodom would have occurred during Abraham's lifetime, which, according to standard Biblical timelines, would be around 1500 years before the exile happened. In Ezekiel 16:49-50, we find the true crime of Sodom and its sister city, Gomorrah: "This was the sin of your sister Sodom: she and her daughters lived in pride, plenty, and thoughtless ease; they neglected the poor and those in need; they grew haughty, and committed idolatries before me and therefore I cast them out of my house."

While we are in the habit of learning from our enemies, let's take a moment to apply my mentor's wisdom here. If there is any unfortunate trait, which Gay men share with the citizens of Sodom, it is not a love of anal intercourse. That was prevalent everywhere! Rather, I would argue that perhaps our arrogance and pride, which encourages us to belittle and demean each other, could be chief among our potential lessons. How many Gay men feel unwelcome in Gay bars and clubs simply because they are not "attractive enough" or young enough? How many older Gay men are taunted by younger Gay men for being out in "the scene" past their prime? How many older Gay men prey on younger men just for their own sexual satisfaction, taking advantage of the financial destitution of the younger men?

The stereotypical selfishness of Gay men and our ability to write each other off, simply because we aren't sexually interested in each other could present us with another lesson. How often do we block each other on hookup sites and apps simply because we're sexually incompatible? How often do we deny friendships with men we find hot, because we "have enough friends" and we're thirsty for romance or, much more likely instead, sex?

Our lack of interest in looking out for each other when we have nothing to gain from the deed could be yet another lesson. How many times in the brief history of the modern Gay Community have Gay men turned our backs on members of the Community who were not sexually desirable to us? This was common during the height of the AIDs crisis, labeling those who were sick as *dirty*, *tainted*, or in some other way *unclean*. Even today, that type of treatment is resurfacing. We turned our backs on the Lesbians who helped us through the AIDs crisis. We're doing it now to Transgender members of the Community.

Ultimately, there are plenty of connections between the behavior of Gay men and the Biblical tale of Sodom, but interpreting the tale as an admonition against anal intercourse between men is disingenuous at best. The city of Sodom was not alone in its acceptance of homosexuality, so if the homophobic Biblical interpretation were correct, every civilization around at the time would have suffered the same fate, not just that one city. Rather, I think that if there is anything for us, as modern Gay men, to learn from the slings and arrows of this particular assault against us, it would be to be kinder and more respectful toward each other.

While the popular modern interpretation of the Abrahamic faiths has always been antagonistic towards homosexuality, not all modern religions have shared that view. For example, Japanese disapproval is far more recent. In fact, as late as 804 C.E. there are documented cases of homosexual relationships between Japanese Buddhist monks and novice male students. These relationships make up a great deal of monastic life for the priests in question.

Today, the Japanese (like the Chinese and the Africans) try to pawn off any instances of homosexuality within their own culture as a Western import. Ironically, it is this distaste for homosexuality, which they imported from the West. As is the case with fashion and architecture, once the Japanese began adopting a more Western attitude, they practically abandoned their own culture. That is why a once noble tradition of homosexuality has been debased as a perversion in their eyes. It's Western imperialism through and through.

Standing in stark contrast to this imported homophobia is a Japanese monastic text called *Kobo Daishi's Book*. Within its pages, the reader will find advice about pederastic homosexuality for the older priests to appeal to when courting novices. It provides graphic details on knowing when a boy is ready to have penetrative sex, and how to coach boys who are not yet ready.

The link between homosexuality and spirituality seems to be universal throughout history. It was only after the West began adopting Christian ideology and the patriarchy began dictating Western morality that attitudes toward homosexuality began to change for the worse. That said, as witches operating in a modern world, we must note that things are necessarily different today than they were in the past, and, we must account for these differences in temperaments, customs, and laws. We must conduct ourselves in line with the laws of the lands where we live.

I wish it were not necessary to make these statements so blatantly, but, not wanting to risk being misunderstood or appear to be advocating something antithetical to my own personal moral code, I will put it plainly in black and white here:

I am NOT advocating pedophilia! Any account of love between an adult man and a boy in this book is academic for the purposes of continuity and context. Anything that was accomplished within a pederastic homosexual relationship in other cultures can and should be modified to account for age of consent laws, the well-being of children, and the betterment of everyone who is mature enough to consent.

In several places in this book, there is talk about homosexual relationships that details the sexual involvement of children, like we have just experienced with Daishi's book. While it is easy for us to judge these individuals or societies as "lecherous" or damaging to these young boys by our own standards of propriety, that was not the case in the context where the events actually occurred.

By all accounts, these ritual acts of homosexuality seem to be consensual, psychologically-affirming, and, in some cases, they were even viewed as necessary rites of passage by everyone within the societies in question. The boys were adequately prepared for the encounter, and they knew what to expect. Even more importantly, they were not taught these encounters were "wrong" from birth or forced to feel shame for having sexual desires after their involvement in these sexual experiences had been revealed.

That said, the same types of historical or anthropological encounters detailed in other cultures are NOT affirming and they are NOT healthy when they are reproduced in our own society today. Our current moral attitudes are directly opposed to teaching any kind of healthy sexuality to children of any age or any sexual orientation—never mind a healthy form of homosexuality! Parents often live blissfully unaware that their children have even a hint of a sexual desire until it becomes impossible to deny the obvious any longer.

Our society does not have the social or political infrastructure necessary to prepare children for the type of transformative psychological experience that these historical accounts are talking about. The way things are currently structured within our society, these types of activities would actually cause grievous mental and/or physical harm to the children involved. The children would most likely experience guilt, shame, and self-loathing from experiences that they are not emotionally or mentally prepared to handle.

Any adult who attempts to justify sex with a minor through the historical accounts detailed in this (or any other) book is delusional and deserves to be prosecuted to the fullest extent of the law. If you're going to include sacred sexuality in your exploration of the Male Mysteries or in your personal magical practice, do it within the confines of the law and be socially responsible.

Make sure that everyone involved is actually in a position to consent—that they are old enough, sober enough, and, generally, aware enough to give consent under any reasonable definition of the term. Look out for your partner's best interest, as well as your own. That's the *perfect love and perfect trust* bit that we witches talk so much about. Be upfront and honest about your sexual health—whether that means revealing your HIV status or the status of another STI, do it! Discuss and honor each other's boundaries, and adhere to best practices for safe sex.

2 MYSTERIOUS MYSTERIES

So ... what exactly are the Male Mysteries as they pertain to Witchcraft?

For that matter, when we talk about the overarching concept of the Gendered Mysteries (Male or Female) within Witchcraft, what are we actually talking about?

In the ancient world, the Mysteries schools were orders of priests and priestesses who sought to attain deeper levels of spiritual wisdom within their given orders. Any witch or magical practitioner who has ever sought initiation into a traditional coven or other Occult Tradition will understand this concept. Most people are familiar with Witchcraft as a fertility (or nature-based) religion. That's certainly its public face, but it's also the easiest aspect of this complex and beautiful spiritual path to grasp when just starting out. However, as you journey down the Crooked Path, deeper occult mysteries reveal themselves to the dedicated initiate.

In *The Republic*, Plato suggests looking at the State to understand the idea of justice and right behavior in the individual. He claims that these things will be easier to see by looking at the larger picture than if you strain to view them on the smaller scale. Personally, if it's good enough for Plato, then it's good enough for me. So, in order to better understand the Male Mysteries (especially as they pertain to Gay men), let's start by taking a look at the overarching concept of Witchcraft and working our way down to the smaller segments of this topic.

The hardest part about discussing Witchcraft in any capacity is that there are so many varieties of it with very little universal consensus between them. When beginning your research into the Old Religion, as it is sometimes called, you will most certainly come across various branches of *Wicca*, which can include coven-based, initiatory traditions, solitary practitioners, and everything in-between. You may also run into *British Traditional Witchcraft* (also called British Traditional Wicca or "BTW"). Another variation on the theme is *Traditional Witchcraft*, which claims to be different than either of the versions just discussed.

That's not even scratching the surface of the confusion, for the record. The public face of Wicca, which you will find online, in some books, and at many festivals can, at times, be drastically different from the coven-based, initiatory variety. Some witches practice exclusively as a spirituality, some as purely a magical practice, and other witches use witchcraft as both. In truth, talking about all witches or all Witchcraft is a bit like talking about all people or all of humanity. It'll be difficult at best.

So, to minimize all this confusion and to avoid unintentionally insulting anyone, I will state my own perspective, which is just that: my perspective. It is how I have come to understand the various branches of the modern Occult Community through my own personal journey. It is certainly not holy writ, and I am not advocating that you must agree with me for this book to work for you. In fact, I am genuinely open to the idea that in time I may come to see things differently. However, because we need a common point to speak from in order to get anywhere in this discussion and because no other universally agreed upon option is available to us, I offer my opinion up as a starting point.

I use the capitalized word *Witchcraft* to refer to all European-derived magical traditions when they are used as a person's spirituality or religion. Personally, I view initiatory, coven-based *Wicca* to be today's version of the ancient world's temple religion. It is where witches who wish to express the priestly calling can learn the prerequisite skills. I view solitary, eclectic, and non-initiatory Wicca, *Traditional Witchcraft*, and *witchcraft* spelled with a lowercase *w* to be folk religion or the craft of casting spells.

As I said, this is only my perspective. It's opinion. If you need to rework any of that for your own purposes, please do.

I tend to agree with Blavatsky and the Theosophists that there was an *Ancient Wisdom Religion*, whose esoteric teachings were the source of all the truth that can be found in the various religions, philosophies, and sciences throughout the world today. Any religion that is valid and uplifting to the human soul will invariably trace its roots back to this Great Knowledge. That being the case, I've never cared much for what things were called, as long as they worked. Besides, witches have always been magpies, collecting bits and bobs from here and there to personalize their practices. I see no reason not to carry on that crafty tradition here and now, simply because it is my own work being repurposed, provided you're fair to it.

My own revelation into the deeper mysteries of Witchcraft came in regard to an issue that many Gay men commonly have with Wicca.

Whenever I talk about Wicca with a group of Gay men, two issues invariably come up. The first is an issue of polarity. The second is Wicca's focus on the feminine to the ostensible exclusion of the masculine.

Considering how polarity has been used against Gay people in the recent past, I completely understand the objection. However, the problem is that you can no more get away from polarity than you can get away from gravity. I know that won't be a popular statement, but just because something is out of fashion or politically incorrect doesn't make it any less true. Truth be told, the *Law of Polarity* has been used to validate Gay people (especially Gay men) far more often than it has been used to ostracize or minimize us. The very roots of our unique and beautiful path are planted in the soil of polarity. There is no getting away from it.

In every historical example where Gay people are honored for our contributions to society, that reverence and respect hinges on polarity. Whether we were medicine men, like some of the Two Spirits, or temple priests, like the gala, our ability to function in that specific role relied on our ability to use the Law of Polarity effectively. Whether we stayed back at camp and helped with maintaining the hearth and home or we went off with a hunting party, our service to the community was contingent upon our ability to play with polarity in unique ways.

While I understand the desire to do away with a concept that is currently being used to harm you, I don't understand the proverbial urge to cut off your nose to spite your face. Railing against polarity, trying to come up with a way to reinvent the wheel simply to avoid dealing with its modern incarnation, or ignoring it altogether—all seem like bad ideas to me, especially when reclaiming our ancestors' perspectives on Gay people and on polarity could be so much more cathartic.

In modern times, polarity's role in the Magical Arts has been expounded upon in numerous volumes. My favorite version of the argument comes from Gavin and Yvonne Frost, because of their implied support of homosexuality within the argument. In their book *The Witch's Magical Handbook* (published in 2000), they confess that it has long been known that the success of a spell requires two people of the opposite gender. Admittedly, that was not groundbreaking. What was groundbreaking, however, was their admission that "opposite gender" did not necessarily mean "opposite sex."

The Frosts are not alone here. Western occult philosophy has a long history of addressing the issue of polarity outside of the confines of gender. Franz Bardon mentions two fundamental and opposite universal energies, which he calls *the magnetic* and *the electric fluids*. Though Bardon uses the *fluid*, what he really means is energy or field. We are not talking about liquids here. In fact, water is attributed to the magnetic current, along with all things that contract, pull in, are passive, or cold. Fire, it's opposite, is attributed to the electric current, along with all that expands, pushes outward, is active, or hot. While a lot of people have push-buttons about having the opposite gender ascribed to them, few people have hang-ups about believing they have two currents or opposite forces working within them. The magnetic and electric of the Western Occult Tradition dissolves a lot of the gender-bias that most people associate with Wicca.

However, as the Frosts insinuate, this is a difficult topic to talk about. A great deal of the frustration that Gay men have with Wicca boils down to this simple fact: English simply does not have the necessary tools to talk about this topic effectively. This shortcoming has produced a lot of unnecessary misunderstanding and confusion.

Once the polarity issue is laid to rest, we still have to contend with the perception that Wicca is highly focused on the Feminine and prejudiced in favor of women. Wicca (and a great deal of Witchcraft) has traditionally been perceived to be focused on the Sacred Feminine, almost, in some cases, to the exclusion or subjugation of the Sacred Masculine. (Whether it actually did exclude or actually did subjugate the Sacred Masculine is a topic for another book.)

When talking strictly about the public image of Wicca (as opposed to what initiated, coven-based witches within healthy traditions experience in their practices), it is the perception that we are most concerned about. The perception seems to be that Wicca focuses on the Feminine to the exclusion of the Masculine. Unfortunately, this perception, whether right or wrong, has turned away many otherwise-interested men from a beautiful religion, which could be of great value to them. In my opinion, that is shameful, and I hope this book does a great deal toward rectifying that injustice.

Within healthy, well-functioning coven-based initiatory Wicca, the roles of men and women are balanced and affirmative of both sexes and both genders. As Tarostar said in his 2015 book *The Sacred Pentagraph*, even the Wheel of the Year finds an equal balance between the opposite poles, alternating Sabbats between the solar or celestial initiation and the terrestrial response to that event. This is part of the Mystery Tradition that lies behind the Fertility Religion, and it rests squarely on the Law of Polarity.

Using the metaphor of the Sun and the Earth in the guise of initiation and response as a key to understanding the energetic currents present in each phase of the seasonal cycles, Tarostar rightly divides the eight seasonal festivals between the two poles—positive and negative, electric and magnetic, and, yes, masculine and feminine. You can choose whatever polarity calls to you, provided you can link it back to nature, and the Wheel would still turn.

Many people take offense at the heteronormative depictions of traditional Wicca and the fact that witches ascribe masculine and feminine traits to what are actually non-gendered forces. On the one hand, the politically correct side of me understands the offense and empathizes with the argument against the model. On the other hand, I absolutely have to concede that it works.

Let's tackle these objections head on.

Many Gay men tend to think of themselves as being outside of the nuclear family construct. However, the simple fact that we are embodied here, on the earthly plane, means that we have (or, at least, had) some part to play within the heterosexual reproductive cycle, no matter how small ... even if that part was only our own births. We cannot get away from the fact that our species engages in heterosexual reproduction. All we can do is explore and understand our actual part within the cycle a bit better.

As for the polarity part of this discussion (beyond what I have already said), every culture and every spiritual tradition on earth has their own way of expressing this wisdom. It's part of that Ancient Wisdom Religion that the Theosophists talk so much about. For the Norse, it was *Frost* and *Fire*. For Taoism, it's the now-ubiquitous concept of *Yin* and *Yang*. The infinity symbol (which looks like a figure 8 turned on its side) hints at polarity.

Even science acknowledges polarity. Within the study of electromagnetism, there is the concept of the dipole, and it is this version of the Law of Polarity that helps explain how magnets are able to do what they do. Newton's third law (for every action, there is an equal and opposite reaction) is subject to polarity. If you want to be successful at magic (or in life), you must acknowledge that you cannot get away from polarity simply because it offends you.

Perhaps it is just the fact that Wicca identifies the concepts of *Male* and *Female* with the two poles that is most offensive to you. You're not so much against polarity, itself, but you're dead-tired of being hit over the head with the heteronormative explanations of it. I feel you there!

The good news?

It really doesn't matter what you label each of the poles. You can make one *Positive* and the other *Negative*. You can choose to designate one pole as *Electric* and the other as *Magnetic*. *Hot* and *Cold* work equally well. It legitimately doesn't matter what you label them as long as they are viewed to be opposites and, within each of those opposites, you can find a hint of the other.

Shifting focus from the Fertility Religion to the Mystery Tradition of Witchcraft, however, actually opens a lot of options for non-heterosexual people to embrace this concept. It allows Gay men (and women) to get out of the heteronormativity of the reproductive cycles that are blatantly portrayed within the most prevalent and public versions of the Wheel of the Year.

When looking at Witchcraft as a Mystery Tradition, I prefer Gavin and Yvonne Frost's understanding of it. For them, Witchcraft (specifically Wicca) is "the Tantra of the West." Slavoj Žižek, a continental philosopher from Slovenia, said, "Our biological body itself is a form of hardware that needs re-programming through tantra like a new spiritual software which can release or unblock its potential." To my mind, this is exactly what Witchcraft does for witches, while they are alive, incarnated in bodies. Witchcraft teaches witches how to use their physical bodies to generate power in order to tap their potential to achieve lasting success in life.

Like Witchcraft, Tantra has no specific, coherent, or overarching doctrine. Instead, it has a method of working. Witches recognize that there are hundreds of ways to cast a circle or work magic, but each coven or tradition has its own documented and proven track record for how they do it. That particular coven's way of doing things certainly won't be for everyone, but it works for them, and that's what matters.

Another connection between Witchcraft and Tantra is their approach to the Mysteries that guide our lives. In probing these Mysteries, the Tantric practitioner, like the witch, seeks to better understand himself, the relationship between people, and the forces that govern all aspects of creation. Most people think that Tantra is about sex, and in all honesty, the detractors of Witchcraft say the same thing about us. The reality is deeper than just that, though. While Tantra can include a sexual component, it is the method of working that makes something Tantric or not, not the sex act itself. The same is true of any particular tradition or practice of Witchcraft.

Since I am not initiated into Tantra, I will refrain from speaking any further on the topic. Concerning Witchcraft, however, I feel comfortable saying that even the most public versions seek to help those who feel drawn to this path to understand themselves better. Once the groundwork of understanding oneself has been accomplished, Witchcraft begins to unfold some of its deeper Tantric-like mysteries for its initiates.

The Female Mysteries are merely one part of the greater Mystery Tradition inherent in the overarching tradition of Witchcraft. The Male Mysteries are another. Remember the Law of Polarity. If we have Female Mysteries, then there must, necessarily, also be Male Mysteries. The archetypal Male is just as powerful, just as mysterious, and just as pervasive as the archetypal Female. Without one, we cannot have the other. This is the piece of the Fertility Religion that all witches need to understand before they can realistically hope to make any real progress within either of the currently-revealed Gendered Mysteries.

The Female Mysteries are far older than their male counterparts. In fact, it has been speculated by some scholars that the oldest forms of magic were tied to women's menstrual cycles. If this theory is true, then men only gained access to these powers later in humanity's evolution.

At their very core, the Female Mysteries are connected to the biological functions of motherhood (menstruating, pregnancy, childbirth, and lactation), and, as such, they are necessarily restricted to women. The Female Mysteries help women in the middle of mothering, and they give purpose to women who have finished raising their children, women who have wisdom to share with the younger generation.

However, there are metaphysical secrets about how the female body works on an energetic level that are also (or, at least, should also be) relayed to women participating in the Female Mysteries, things like how to work with the Feminine Polarity, how to balance it with the Masculine Polarity, how to use menstrual blood to good effect, how to embrace their potential to nurture life through their bodies, etc., and what these things mean on a magical or energetic level.

Modern Witchcraft's public focus on the Goddess is a direct result of these Mysteries. The Feminine is seductive. To use an old occult term, it is magnetic. Naturally, it would be the Feminine that would become the public face of the witch's path. It's welcoming! It draws in, and it is the warm comfort of the Mother.

However, the archetypal Feminine is not just the Mother's warm embrace. She is also the void, and the force that pulls us back into the void. Take, for example, the myth about *The Rape of Persephone*. Demeter is the Grain Mother who nurtures all living things. She is the archetypal Feminine force of caregiving and compassion, but when her beloved daughter, Persephone, is stolen from her, she grieves and makes the world grieve right along with her. Her magnetism is so powerful that it forces the first winter, which, to my mind, accounts for so much more than just an explanation of the creation of the seasons. It also hints at secrets within the Female Mysteries, which are only known to its initiates.

While many can see the mysteries of the female biology, most lack the eyes to see the corresponding mysteries of the male. That does not mean that they don't exist. It only means that the Male Mysteries have been so well-hidden for so long that people tend to overlook them.

3 MALE MYSTERIES

Taking our cue from Plato, let's start by looking at the Male Mysteries from a broad, overarching metaphysical perspective and work our way down. Perhaps the very place to start with that endeavor is with a myth that has become nearly universal among modern witches. The Italian witches' myth regarding Aradia's birth, which was recorded by Charles G. Leland, reveals more about the Male Mysteries than any other myth.

According to Leland, Diana was created before everything else, and she divided herself into two opposites—darkness and light. In the division of these two opposites, Lucifer, who was her brother, her son, and her other half, was the light. When Diana saw that the light was beautiful, she yearned "with great desire" to reconnect with it, but Lucifer fled from her. Diana went to "the fathers of Beginning, to the mothers, the spirits who were before the first spirit," and she lamented her situation. They praised her and told her that she must humble herself, that to become the chief of goddesses, she must become mortal.

Both Lucifer and Diana were humbled as the ancestors decreed. Lucifer fell.[3] Diana went on earth to teach magic and sorcery. In truth, both of them "fell." The original myth says that they humbled themselves. Rather than see fire and brimstone in Lucifer, as the Christians are wont to do, I find it hard not to notice a similarity with the Biblical Jesus and his crucifixion here. The humbling of Diana and Lucifer is where the first witches came from according to the Aradia Myth.

It happened that Diana prevailed with Lucifer's beloved pet cat to switch forms with her. The cat slept on Lucifer's bed each night, and Diana wanted the opportunity to get closer to her brother. In the darkness, Diana assumed her own form again, and, by laying with her brother, she became the mother of Aradia.

Through the mythic language of metaphor and symbol, this story

---

[3] The bible has a perverted version of this part of the myth, but certain wisdom can still be gleaned by looking past the typical Christian judgement.

reveals a great deal about the Male Mysteries to those who know where to look. As I have already said, the Female Mysteries are far older than the Male. In the Aradia Myth, this can be seen when we look at Diana, who was, as Leland said, created first.

The fact that Diana is associated with the darkness and Lucifer is associated with the light is no mere accident. The light seems to be a universal symbol for the male, and it holds countless mysteries about the Masculine Polarity. (We'll get to those in the next chapter.)

Lucifer's desire to maintain his independence from Diana is another piece of the puzzle. His almost pathological fear of having his light extinguished by her darkness hints at the male ego's desire for legacy, permanence, structure, and, ultimately, order. The darkness, then, is symbolic of the void and chaos, which terrifies him.

However, as is the fate of all light, Lucifer's light actually does get extinguished by Diana's darkness in the myth. For the gods, it happens when they embrace in sexual union. However, candles eventually burn out, letting darkness creep in, and even stars die, leaving only darkness in their wake. I believe that the French got it right when they referred to the orgasm as "la petite morte" or *the little death*, and Lucifer, being avaricious in nature, seems reluctant to concede even that much of his existence in this myth.

I have a theory for you to mull over as you read the rest of this book. It is only a theory, but I have yet to disprove it for myself, and I think pondering it can only help someone who wishes to embrace the Male Mysteries more fully. Perhaps it is the secret knowledge of the male's fragility, which the orgasm reveals as the ego loses hold on itself, that is the cause of patriarchy's hatred of sex. In sex's climax, man lets himself go, and, in that brief moment of oblivion, he realizes his fate.

The Italian witches were not alone in their cosmology. Even modern philosophy, with its staunch reliance on reason and logic, seems to back up the historic wisdom of the Italian witches. In 1979, Jean Baudrillard published his book *Seduction*, espousing the witchiest philosophy to grace the ivory tower since Friedrich Nietzsche honored Apollo and Dionysus in *The Birth of Tragedy*.

Baudrillard understands the Law of Polarity in a way that few modern witches do. In fact, in many respects the way he chooses to label the two poles in his philosophy appears far more balanced at first blush than anything we, witches, have put forth publicly. Baudrillard labels the two poles *Production* and *Seduction*.

Production is the force that brings order out of chaos. Seduction is the force that reverses or undoes that order. Witches, on the other hand, tend to talk about the two poles as *Masculine-Feminine, Male-Female, God-Goddess*, which is all perfectly balanced and lovely, but then we also go on to use loaded phrases like *Positive-Negative, Creation-Destruction, Order-Chaos, Light-Dark*.

We can profess to the high heavens that *Negative, Destructive, Chaos,* and *Dark(ness)* do not mean *Bad*, but people new to the Craft, who have not spent time deciphering our symbols, read these phrases "negatively," and it hinders them. In fact, society has a huge investment in continuing to qualify these things as actually being *Bad*. We can talk about the Negative Pole as if it were one end of a battery all we want, and, though we are 100% correct, most people will immediately equate *Negative* with *Bad*. It is only after a moment of translation that they will overcome the habit.

Witches know that destruction can be beautiful, but how many people drive themselves crazy attempting to avoid the ravages of time? How many people fight the effects of aging tooth and nail? How many struggle to maintain financial empires, or protect real estate from natural disasters? There really isn't any place in our modern society that we don't fight the forces of destruction. Entire industries have been built up around bringing order to chaos. The insurance industry, for example, continues to thrive on the fears surrounding the general public's obsession with loss, grief, and destruction.

Most people tend to be afraid of the dark. Some bigoted people believe that darker skin tones make one less attractive. Society puts in a lot of effort to back up and maintain its prejudices.

Personally, I feel that this effort of translation is a small price to pay for real power. I would also encourage anyone struggling with this issue to resolve it to their satisfaction as quickly as possible. You don't have to like it for something to be true; but, ignoring the truth simply because you dislike it is a recipe for failure. Furthermore, rethinking ideas that have been ingrained in us is one of the hallmarks of a true witch. That's part of the "to know" piece of *The Witch's Pyramid*. It's also the theory behind old-school covens making people say the Lord's Prayer backwards. Can you overcome your own prejudices and fears in order to see things as they really are? If so, then the path of the witch might be for you. If not, then perhaps you need something different.

However, I also understand the value of tools. Few children learn to ride bikes without training wheels, and most successful witches acknowledge the value of their athames, wands, and brooms to their magical practices. If less-loaded words help you get over this hurdle in the beginning, then I think it would be appropriate to search out words and symbols that work for you and your practice. Baudrillard makes an excellent case for *Production* and *Seduction*, and the various ways these two concepts line up with current Witchcraft theory are endless.

Now, you may argue that *Seduction* is not, in fact, any less loaded a word than words like *Negative*, *Destructive*, *Chaos*, or *Dark(ness)*, and while I will agree with you in some respects, it does lack the necessity of immediate translation that each of the other labels brings along with them. All people seduce. Though it is "softer" and subtler than a fight or an all-out-war, in many ways, seduction was considered a "masculine art" for the bulk of its history. In fact, its emasculation is a relatively recent occurrence.

Many wealthy families built their houses upon seduction's foundations. The Tudors, the Habsburgs, the Plantagenets all cleared the way for their empires with the use of seduction. The Habsburg motto publicly declared their love of seduction: "Let others wage war, but you, happy Austria, shall marry." The Medici and the Rothschild families both used seduction to consolidate power in the financial sphere.

Beyond the more progressive stance on gender, we often talk about seduction like it is, in fact, a good thing. While patriarchy and Christianity do their level best to establish seduction as an evil or underhanded art, we still have plenty of examples of its equally positive qualities. (For the record, anything that seduction suffers under Christianity and patriarchy, witchcraft also suffers—they are the same thing.) Baudrillard says, "For religion seduction was a strategy of the devil, whether in the guise of witchcraft or love."[4]

Couples who inspire us to be more loving are seen to seduce (or romance) each other. Companies spend millions of dollars on marketing (mass seduction), providing countless people with jobs. Sales is just a more intimate form of professional seduction than marketing. Even the modern science of psychology is more successful when it embraces seductive techniques (like active listening, repeating back what was said, reframing unpleasant events to view them

---

[4] Baudrillard, Jean. *Seduction*. New World Perspectives, 1990, p. 1.

differently, etc.).

For Baudrillard, production belongs to the realm of nature. Production provides structure, meaning, and order. Discrimination and the ability to discern, to make distinctions are its preferred strategies, hence our society's infinitely-distracting obsession with reason and science. Nietzsche ascribed these traits to the *Apollonian*, which he named after another god of light.

It seems counter-intuitive (when compared against the word *seduction*), but things like sex and desire are within production's purview, not seduction's. This is especially true when sex and desire can be studied, catalogued, and managed.

Language and discourse are the primary tools used to produce anything. Even the Christian *Bible* honors this universal truth. God speaks to bring about nature. "And God said, 'Let there be light,' and there was light." It is language that gave the Christian God his patriarchal power over nature in *Genesis*.

As magical people, we buy into this concept as well—hook, line, and sinker. Have you ever noticed that patriarchal religions and the magical systems that stem from them exhaust themselves worrying about names and the act of knowing something's name, like a real-life Rumpelstiltskin drama? If you label something, you can control it, you can put it within a structure or a cosmic order. In Baudrillard's terminology, it is the force of production at work here! By knowing his name, the Miller's daughter was able to control all that Rumpelstiltskin had done and restore order out of his chaos.

Even witchcraft (a matriarchal path in any of its incarnations) agrees with Baudrillard's assessment of production. To see this, simply take another look at the Aradia Myth. It is Lucifer's separation from Diana that brought nature into existence. It is the moment that the male came into being, which initiated the process of ordering chaos.

Prior to the separation, Diana and Lucifer (just called *Diana* in the myth) were outside of nature. Leland tells us this by saying, "Diana was the first created before all creation."[5] Together, they were something else, indistinct, unknowable, and unable to be produced—some witches call this union *Dryghtyn*. It is the order of the male[6] that brings about the natural world through the Law of Polarity, with all its

---

[5] Leland, Charles G. *Aradia or Gospel of the Witches*. The Career Press, Inc., 2003, p. 41.
[6] Baudrillard actually does associate production with the male, just as the Aradia myth does.

distinctions and separations.

Baudrillard says, "All masculine power is a power to produce. All that is produced, be it the production of woman as female, falls within the register of masculine power."[7] Diana as a separate and distinct entity, a woman made female, is produced by the exception of Lucifer from Dryghtyn.

After the one becomes two, all that became Lucifer was removed from the whole. Diana, as we understand her, came into being when all that remained behind coalesced into something else, namely, the Goddess we all know and love. He was light, so she was dark.

We have a tendency to think of femininity as the opposite of masculinity, but it is not. The femininity, which we place opposite masculinity is still a construct laid out by the male for the benefit of the male. The true feminine reveals itself through uncertainty. The two spirit, the mahus, and the gala priests of history all knew this, and they claimed it as a cornerstone of their power. Baudrillard says that true femininity abolishes the differential opposition between the masculine and the feminine entirely.

Look at Diana seeking to reunite with her brother. Look at her desire to receive the light back into her darkness, to make the two of them whole again. Baudrillard says, "It is not quite feminine as surface that is opposed to masculine as depth, but the feminine as indistinctness of surface and depth."[8] Diana, as a separate and individual "embodied" female goddess is not opposed to Lucifer. She is his compliment. What we call *Dryghtyn* (and the Italian witches labeled *Diana* prior to the split) stands in opposition to Lucifer. This is the true power of femininity, of the female, and we find it in full-force within the Aradia Myth.

Most witches tend to think of Dryghtyn as just slightly more male than female. Though they may not acknowledge the truth in that statement, the very name used to refer to the concept betrays the bias. *Dryghtyn* is an Old English term, which means *Lord*. In truth, Dryghtyn, *The Prime Mover*, *The One*, *Great Spirit*, *God* (whatever you want to call it) would not be male. All gender differentials would disappear from it completely, leaving something indistinct, unknowable, and "seductive" in place of the two former opposites, something truly feminine!

---

[7] Baudrillard, Jean. *Seduction*. New World Perspectives, 1990, p. 15.
[8] Baudrillard, Jean. *Seduction*. New World Perspectives, 1990, p. 10.

As I have said before, the Female Mysteries are older than the Male. What I have not said in so many words yet is that in addition to being older, the Female Mysteries (and the Female as an archetypal force) will outlast the Male. Perhaps this is why the Italian witches so cleverly chose to name the unified Godhead as *Diana* prior to the appearance of Lucifer.

Baudrillard tells us that seduction has no power of its own, except that it annuls the forces of production.[9] However, seduction always succeeds at undoing production. As witches, we have other resources that point to the truth of this statement. We often talk about all power coming from the God, but the Goddess being able to "strap on the sword when the need arises."

Even older accounts of the Goddess pay homage to this theory as well. Cybele's intersex birth (in her Agdistis path) is a common part of her overarching mythology. Her penis was cut off, because the other gods feared the power that the indistinctness of gender gave her. Ishtar has similar elements of indistinctness regarding gender in her own mythologies. Even the earliest representations of Isis (specifically Isis-Net or Isis when she is paired with Anat) were viewed to be both male and female, or at the very least androgynous/gynandrous. The feminine is actually more like Cybele, Ishtar, or Isis than it is like more common Goddess imagery. The feminine is indistinctness of gender or sex. What we call *feminine* is only our feeble attempt to understand something unfathomable. She exists beyond polarity, outside of nature, and eternally!

Baudrillard and the Italian witches seem to agree. The pole, which we, witches, label *Feminine* and he labels *Seduction*, stands as a challenge to the pole we label *Masculine* and he labels *Production*. The Feminine stands as a constant challenge to the thing produced should it endeavor to remain, like the tide challenges the beach. And, like the dunes, which many coastal towns set up to fend off the chaos of the sea, the Masculine sets up what Baudrillard calls a *"phallic fortress"* to protect itself from the dark forces of chaos and destruction. Like all fortresses, the phallic fortress of the masculine polarity betrays the weakness it tries to conceal. If the holding weren't vulnerable to attack in the first place, there would never have been a need to build the fortress to protect it.

---

[9] Baudrillard, Jean. *Seduction*. New World Perspectives, 1990, p. 15.

Baudrillard puts forth a theory, which is central to both of the Gendered Mysteries. "One can hypothesize that the feminine is the only sex, and the masculine only exists by a superhuman effort to leave [the feminine]. A moment's distraction and the masculine falls back into the feminine."[10]

We can see this in the Aradia Myth. Lucifer fights so hard for his independence, and the moment he takes rest and falls back on his comfortability, Diana reclaims what was taken from her. This is the secret that any man who wishes to explore the Male Mysteries must fully reconcile for himself. This secret explains why the great bulk of witches (and, in truth, most magically-talented people) tend to be female, or, if they are male by sex, they tend to be feminine in some other way. The more one staunchly clings to his masculinity or willingly falls within the masculine structures set up by society (whatever that means to him or her), the less open that individual will be to the magic, which exists beyond the walls of the phallic fortress. This truth is also engraved above the very threshold of the phallic fortress, which bars the way for men who cling to their masculinity and their identity as 100% heterosexual males. It is the reason why there needs to be Gay Male Mysteries instead of just Male Mysteries within our culture.

---

[10] Baudrillard, Jean. *Seduction*. New World Perspectives, 1990, p. 16.

4 PHALLIC FORTRESS

"STRING!!!" I screamed at the top of my little 5 year old lungs. Every muscle in my body had tightened up, like rigor mortis setting in—every muscle, that is, except the ones connected to my mouth. (I'm sure my family did not appreciate the irony of that, by the way.) My mom came running into the room, like she had done countless times before, to pull the offending string off of my sock, or shirt, or pants, or from wherever it might have dangled.

"Honestly, Casey!" she said, justifiably exacerbated by the absurdity of the situation. "It's only a stupid piece of string!" She quickly snapped the string free of the garment, and, just like that, I was fine again. It was as if the fibrous threat had never existed in the first place.

Years later, my aunt found an article in the paper discussing linaphobia (or the fear of unraveling). Suddenly, my family had a name for this very weird and quirky pattern of behavior that I had exhibited as a child. It wasn't just me being needy or "special." I had suffered from a real fear. Apparently, according to the article, every time I saw a piece of string dangling from my clothes, I thought it was an extension of myself. (The string never seemed to bother me if it was laying on the ground or was connected to someone else's clothing.) As I looked at the string dangling precariously off of my body, I became imminently aware of my own potential unraveling.

Whenever I read the Aradia Myth, I often wonder if Lucifer didn't experience some cosmic version of linaphobia when confronted with the possibility of reuniting with Diana. Did he fear that reunification was tantamount to going back into the void and undoing all that had been done, all that gave him his independent existence?

This rather humorous tale from my own childhood illustrates another interesting point, which we should consider. If the male is so fragile, why would anyone aspire to handicap themselves further by engaging in the Male Mysteries at all? Wouldn't it be better to help people embrace the truth and move beyond the illusion of separateness by embracing the Feminine instead?

Arguably, that is what all valid religions do. Even the most patriarchal religions have the truth of the feminine buried deep within them. "Love your neighbor as yourself." Matthew 22:39 encourages us to embrace indistinctness between ourselves and our neighbors, encouraging compassion and a welcoming nature—all things that most witches would ascribe to the Feminine pole within the Law of Polarity.

That is, after all, a secret of the law. As I hinted before, the opposites are not completely separated or divorced from each other. Like the Yin-Yang symbol, each has the other within it.

The Male Mysteries are no different. In fact, it is yet another misconception that the Male Mysteries celebrate the male state. Certainly, the Male Mysteries acknowledge the value of the archetypal Male and seek to enable men to live better lives as men, but no truth can be blind to the realities of the world. The Male Mysteries account for the weaknesses inherent in the male state (weaknesses we saw in Baudrillard's philosophy), and these mysteries enable men to strengthen their position by embracing the feminine within the masculine. Even Odin had to embrace the feminine within himself so that he could gain access to his shamanic powers.

The Male Mysteries hold three symbols sacred above all others, because they remind us of this truth. The first of these symbols is the Blacksmith, who stands as the archetypal alchemist, transmuting the power of the female for the use of men. The second symbol is the crossroads, which represents the transition out of the void into nature, and the third symbol is the light, which constantly labors to hold back the darkness.

Just as Lucifer was born out of the process of separating from Diana and the light emerged from the darkness, the Male Mysteries evolved out of the Female Mysteries. In her *Element Encyclopedia of Witchcraft*, Judika Illes claims that the process of transferring magic away from women towards men started with the art of metalworking, and I would venture to say that she is probably correct.

The basic theory goes like this: prior to the iron age, magic was the exclusive domain of women, as they were the only people who produced menstrual blood, and menstrual blood was a central component of most magical systems at the time. However, once iron was discovered, and people learned how to forge it, men (the blacksmiths) gained access to magic. They were working with the menstrual blood of the Great Mother, and it gave them all the powers claimed traditionally by women. As male blacksmiths got their hands on this potent substance, they became more than just artisans; they became master magicians and priests of the Earth.[11]

Today, we treat blacksmithing as a fun hobby or an eccentric pastime. Very few people have the time or freedom to learn the skill in a traditional way anymore, and even fewer people could afford to set themselves up as a blacksmith full-time and make enough money to sustain a modern lifestyle. That wasn't always the case, though. Throughout history, all the way back to the beginning of the Iron Age, the blacksmith was one of the most essential members of society. In addition to smithing iron, the blacksmith also served as the dentist, barber, tattoo artist, and healer (which even included functioning as a surgeon from time to time) for his community—all those skills needing either the knowledge he learned or the materials he made at the forge.

This central role and his connection to healing (especially with herbs) led the blacksmith to explore magic and ritual in addition to his mundane tasks. Over time, he became adept at tending to the community in these various ways, and a folklore built up around the profession.

To see the blacksmith's connection to magic, you only have to look at the world's many mythologies surrounding the archetype. A recurring theme across countless cultural myths is the lame or disfigured blacksmith. On the most basic level, the injured leg makes the smith a *wounded healer*, someone who can survive and even thrive after the wound has been inflicted.

Wounded healer is often a term used to describe shamanic practitioners the world over. On a more metaphorical level, the wounded leg symbolizes the fact that the smith has one foot in the world of man and one foot in the spirit world. This ability to function within two worlds simultaneously is often attributed to shamans, witches, and other magical practitioners.

Hephaestus, from Greek mythology, is the most famous example of this archetype, but there are others. Wayland the Smith, who was hamstrung by the evil King Nidung so that he could not leave the kingdom, fills this role in Germanic mythology. Kothar, who was known by his "distinctive walk," was the ancient West Semitic god of crafts. In Zulu mythology, the god Ngungi sacrifices one of his eyes and his leg to gain knowledge.

The connection between a deep and lasting wound and shamanic

---

[11] Illes, Judika. *Element Encyclopedia of Witchcraft*. Harper Collins Publishers, 2005, p. 632.

spirits can be seen in countless cultures. Like Ngungi, Odin sacrifices his own eye for knowledge. Osiris, in Egypt, was originally a fertility god who became Lord of the Dead (a very shamanic calling, indeed!) after being killed and dismembered by his brother, Set. Before she resurrected him, Isis (Osiris's wife and sister) searched the land for her husband's scattered body parts. She was successful in finding all of them, except his phallus, which was thrown into the Nile and eaten by an elephant fish.

Though most modern versions of the Dionysian myths do not focus on his shamanic qualities, Dionysus also has some definite shamanic associations. During his first incarnation, as Zagreus, Dionysus was born to Persephone and Zeus. During that lifetime, he was viciously torn apart by the Titans. Many shamans talk about being twice born or being torn apart during their initiatory process. My own dream where the God removed my kidneys is a personal example of this. You might have your own.

Like Osiris, Zagreus's phallus was removed from his body during his dismemberment. Unlike Osiris, however, Zagreus's phallus was recovered. Two dwarves recovered the discarded phallus and deposited it in a cave on the Isle of Samothrake, establishing a shrine for the dead god. (Those dwarves were sons of Hephaestus and also blacksmiths in their own right.) Zeus recovered Zagreus's heart and made it into a potion, which he fed to Semele, who then gave birth to Dionysus. In one of the later myths, which we will explore further on in this book, Dionysus journeys into the Underworld to rescue his mother from Death and bring her back to Mount Olympus, which is extremely shamanic.

The blacksmith, more than any other archetype, gives men access to true power. He transmutes the Female Mysteries for the use of men, but he also transmutes weakness into strength. It is only by embracing the weakened state, the wound or disfigurement, that we can become strong, that we can thrive. Rather than see this disfigurement or dismemberment as a detriment to his strength or power, the archetype of the shamanic blacksmith teaches us how to turn what seems like a disadvantage into a source of power.

The value of the crossroads to the Male Mysteries can be seen in the Aradia Myth. Leland describes that pivotal moment when Diana and Lucifer separate into two distinct beings. Within the realm of the Male Mysteries, this is the liminal moment of creation, the moment when the male came into being. He was born out of the liminal. She existed both before and after that liminal moment. For witches, liminality is often represented as a crossroads, and it is for that reason that the Male Mysteries revere the crossroads so highly.

Prior to Diana and Lucifer separating, they were both something else. They were presumably Dryghtyn. What were they in that brief moment that they were neither purely Dryghtyn anymore but they were not quite Diana and Lucifer either? This is an essential question that all who venture down the Male Mystery path towards this particular intersection must eventually ask. It is the crossroads that reminds us of that liminal threat to our existence and the very possibility of production.

The crossroads is symbolic of both creation and destruction within the Male Mysteries. It invokes the powers that brought this world into creation, but it also hides the forces that can undo all that was produced. Whenever the crossroads shows up as a theme within the various world mythologies, it carries the weight of this reality behind it.

We can see this dual nature play out in some of the oldest folklore attached to crossroads. In every instance where the crossroads appears, it has both a positive and a negative component. It is, in itself, neutral (yet another form of liminality), and, being neutral, it potentially brings both forces to bear on the person who invokes its power.

The living journey to these intersections to engage or dissuade the dead. In the United Kingdom, they used to bury criminals and people who committed suicide outside the city limits at a crossroads, because they believed that the possibilities represented by the intersection would confuse the dead and protect the living from their baneful influence.

As witches, we claim the crossroads as our personal domain. It is where we go to cast some of our most powerful spells and eliminate the remains of things that no longer serve us. Geomancy (with its ley lines) holds the key to unlocking this value of crossroads for witches. It is not just the fact that these spaces are betwixt and between that makes them special, though that certainly helps. Science is beginning to validate what we witches have known for so long: there is a real world, physical reason why these intersections hold the influence that they do.

On a purely scientific level,[12] a ley line is a straight fault line, a crack in the earth's tectonic plates. These cracks release powerful magnetic energies, which sensitive people can feel.

On a metaphysical level, this information makes the crossroads a bit like the symbol of the blacksmith for any witch pursuing the Male Mysteries. With the blacksmith, it is the Earth Mother's secretions (iron), which propels the Mystery forward. In the case of the crossroads, it is her magnetism. Either way, the Male Mysteries owe a debt of gratitude to the Female Mysteries, which preceded them.

Aspirants of every stripe attend these special spots to produce undeveloped talents within themselves. Unfortunately, as some of the stories go, they must sell their souls to do it. The most famous example of this exists in Blues Music. Most people talk about Robert Johnson journeying to the crossroads with his guitar to barter his soul for musical talent from the Man in Black. Others say it was Tommy Johnson. For our purposes, it doesn't much matter either way. The point is the same.

The mythology surrounding the production of talent associated with the crossroads is so powerful that modern day artists are taking it to heart. The list of people who have made this particular pact with the famed Man in Black is numerous. It includes artists, musicians, actors, writers, business men, politicians, and nearly any other member of society you can name.

The light stands as the third symbol of the Male Mysteries. The connection between the light and the Male exists in science as well as mythology. When you consider that the light is not just electromagnetic waves, that, yes, it is heat and illumination, but it is also beauty, fascination, and the object of sight, you can see why mythologies the world over have associated this sign with the Male or Masculine Polarity.

The fact that Lucifer's beauty fascinated Diana and held her entranced for as long as it did is a central piece of the Male Mysteries. We see this concept played out in nature all the time. The male of the species is flashier, using his beauty to distract predators from his duller, female mate. Fascination and glamour are tools of the Male. Humans

---

[12] Unfortunately, I must admit that this science is a "pseudo-science," because all talk of anything spiritual or magical is viewed with derision by most mainstream branches of science. However, I have no doubt that much of what is currently being labeled "pseudo-science" will, eventually, lead to major breakthroughs that "real" science cannot ignore.

are the only animals who topple the natural order by having women preen and primp the way we do.

Male cardinals are a vibrant red. The female of the species wears a dull brown. The male peacock sports that brilliant blue-green we all know and love, and he has that gorgeous train. His mate is far more subdued. The peahen has brown, gray, or cream colored feathers to camouflage her. The male elephant (in Asia) has his ivory tusks. The female doesn't. Bucks have antlers; does do not. Male lions have that beautiful mane, whereas the lioness is bald.

On a very basic level, this truth is a matter of evolution and survival. The male has a small part to play in rearing the offspring. Once his contribution is over (generally speaking), he is free to walk away ... or, at the very least, his mobility isn't hindered. The female may have a nest to watch after or a birthing process to endure. More to the point, in species with intrauterine births, if the female is hunted or killed, both her and the offspring would be lost. Having the male of the species draw attention away from her and the offspring ensures the survival of the species.

This evolutionary survival tactic is not just a matter of science. It has its roots within the mythic sphere as well. Its roots as a male construct take hold in metaphysical soil with the various lords of light. Generally, the god of light is beautiful, but he also tends to be the force that brings order out of chaos. Sometimes, as we saw with Lucifer, he is even connected with the creation of the natural order.

The Greek myths, and eventually Nietzsche, credited Apollo with this function. Apollo was said to be the most beautiful of the Greek Gods, and he was credited with a divine knowledge so powerful it transcended into wisdom (both oracular and otherworldly).

Within the traditional philosophical canon, production's connection to the Light as an archetypal symbol can be seen most blatantly in Friedrich Nietzsche's *The Birth of Tragedy*. Nietzsche uses the concepts of the Dionysian and the Apollonian to designate two central principles of Greek culture. The Dionysian breaks down individuality. (In Baudrillard's theory, the Dionysian would be seductive, which accounts for much of the feminine portrayals of Dionysus in both myth and art.) The Dionysian is ecstasy (orgasm), madness, drunkenness, and even enthusiasm. All the places where we "lose ourselves" in life. The Apollonian, on the other hand, corresponds to individuation. It is diametrically opposed to the

Dionysian, and it stands in for clarification, demarcation, delineation, and formalization in Nietzsche's concept. It is reason and the rational. It is the very basis for the analytical quality that we prize so highly in the West. (In Baudrillard's theory, it is the real and it is all things produced.)

In a great many of the world's mythologies, the Light symbolizes the forces of production and is represented by a male god, intimately connected to reason (or some other form of production). In Celtic mythology, there is Lugh, who was said to be knowledgeable and skilled in every art. Amun-Ra from Egypt is another example. He was originally two gods who merged into one—the first, a deity of Air; the second being associated with the Sun or Light. Amun has been translated as "hidden," "invisible," "mysterious," whereas Ra gets translated as "light." For modern people, the hidden light of knowledge is so commonplace that we use it to define whole periods of time when knowledge was either prized or loathed (The Age of Enlightenment, The Dark Ages, etc.). In Norse mythology, there is Baldr, who is god of many things, including light. The Māori have Ao, who is a god of light and the land of the living. Hindu mythology has Agni as the god of fire and one of many sun gods.

Lucifer, being the most widely-talked about Lord of Light in the modern era (mostly due to misguided and incorrect Biblical associations of him with Satan), deserves some mention here. We have already seen how the Italian witches treated Lucifer, through Leland's lens, but they were not alone in their worship of this luminescent spirit. In Greece and Rome, he was honored as Eosphorus (or Phosphorus), the light bringer, connected to the Morning and Evening Star (Venus). In the Theogony, Hesiod says that Eosphorus was born to Eos (the Dawn) and Astraeus (the Starry). Another source claims that Eosphorus was born to Eos (Aurora in Latin) and Cephalus, whose beauty rivaled even Venus, herself. For the Yazidis, Lucifer is recognized as Melek Taus, the Peacock Angel. Even within the Judeo-Christian context, you can find positive associations for Lucifer if you look beyond the traditional canon into the *Apocrypha*. In Enoch, for example, we see the angel Lumiel (another name for Lucifer) as the protector of the Earth as well as the bearer of light.

The light is so much more than just beauty, intelligence, and illumination, though. Like staring into the bright glare of the noonday sun, the light can obscure as much as it can reveal. Within Hindu mythology, this concept is called *Maya*.

Maya, for the Hindu faith has been translated as many things. First, it was viewed to be the magical power associated with a god or goddess. It has been translated as *delusion, trickery, fraud,* and *deceit*. However, most often *Maya* has been translated as *illusion of the world*.

According to Vedic texts, this world that we live in is a distraction, an illusion, something meant to be seen through to the reality beneath. It fascinates and holds us in awe so that we cannot see beyond it without real effort. Ultimately, Maya is caused by an imperfect, discriminating, intelligence, because it is the individual self, which can be deceived, not the eternal spirit or soul. I am endlessly-fascinated by how all of this meshes up! Individuality, discernment, reason, discrimination, the light, illusion (or magic), the masculine polarity—whether we're talking philosophy, science, or mythology, this pole within the Law of Polarity seems to bear a distinctive hallmark regardless of the veneer placed over it, and it is that hallmark that seems to give the Male Mysteries their currency.

This connection between illusion, fascination, and the archetypal Male exists in other cultures as well. Our English word *fascination* even bears this connection out in black and white. According to the *American Heritage Dictionary*, our modern word *fascinate* can mean "To capture and hold the interest and attention of. / 2. Archaic: To deprive of the ability to escape or move, usually by the power of a look. Used of serpents. / 3. Obsolete: To bewitch."

Fascinate derives from the Latin word *fascinare*, which, itself derives from the much older Latin word *fascinum*. In Latin, *fascinare* is generally agreed to have meant "to cast a spell on," and, once again, like in the case of Maya, we are seeing the connection between the Male Polarity and magic.

There are various translations of *fascinare*, depending on the dictionary you consult, but they are all variations on a theme. The *Latin to English Dictionary* defines *fascinare* simply as "bewitch." The *Dictionary of the Royal Academy of the Spanish Language* says *fascinare* included the concepts "1. Deceive, to hallucinate, obfuscate. / 2. Attract irresistibly / 3. Make evil eye."

It is the older word *fascinum*, which most concerns us here in our discussion of the Male Mysteries. *Fascinum* (alternatively *fascinus*) meant "enchantment, spell, or witchcraft" like the later *fascinare*. However, this more archaic word also described a phallic-shaped charm, which hung around the necks of children to protect them from the evil eye.

Pliny tells us that the fascinum charm could also be placed in the garden and on hearths to protect oneself against the fascinations of the envious (the evil eye). Incidentally, in his *Onomasticon*, Pollux tells us that blacksmiths hung the fascinum charm before their forges for the same purpose. While some cultures, I'm specifically thinking of the Norse here (but there are others), believed witchcraft to be "women's work," a thorough study of the concept of fascination demonstrates a very real connection between witchcraft and the Male Polarity.

As a funny little side note to prove the connection between this concept and the human male, let's look at a particularly interesting bit of modern urban slang, which has inherited fascination's phallic legacy. Have you ever heard of someone being "dickmatized" by a man's penis? At its most basic level, being dickmatized involves someone being obsessed with a penis, though the phrase has been used to explain otherwise puzzling behaviors as well. The *Urban Dictionary* defines the concept as "when the dick makes you say/do crazy things."

What this urban slang demonstrates is that even today, the connection between the phallus and fascination is intuitively understood by people who most likely have no knowledge of the intimate history behind this relationship. Beyond this rather humorous colloquial usage, we find plenty of connections between fascination and the phallus within more mainstream sources. From the mythology of the Mediterranean tradition, we find ithyphallic deities, who blatantly express this connection. Among the most famous are Fascinus, Priapus, Pan, and Silvanus.

The link between fascination and the phallus is probably made most explicit with the Mediterranean god Fascinus, who is actually personified by the phallus, itself. Not much is known about this god, but it is his representation as the phallus, and his dominion over good luck, witchcraft, and breaking curses, especially the evil eye (which all fall under the fascination umbrella) that is important to us here.

There were plenty of other phallic deities of fascination within the Mediterranean tradition who share this link. For example, the word *panic* is derived from a connection to the Greek God Pan. When you consider that the essence of fascination is to irresistibly draw and maintain the interest and attention of someone, it is easy to see that fascination does not always have to be enjoyable. There is nothing innately built into the definition that speaks of pleasure, joy, or exclusively positive qualities. Terror can also be fascinating in this sense. When you are terrified, your attention is held captive by the object of the fear you are experiencing. You are fascinated!

Silvanus, the Roman God of the forest who watched over the wilderness, is another phallic god. A simple connection between Silvanus and the phallus is the fact that he is a horned spirit. Horns can mean many things in mythology. They can express power. They can connect a deity with the rays of the sun, but beneath all those associations lies a deeper, intimate connection with the phallus. Any horned spirit is expressing some ithyphallic connection. There are plenty of spirits (male and female) that display horns, but, in each case, this display is meant to indicate a power to produce in some way.

While Priapus is not a horned spirit, like Silvanus, his connection to the phallus is much more obvious. In fact, this connection was so strong that our modern word *priapic*, which means "relating to or resembling a phallus," comes from his name. His influence has even branched out into modern medicine. *Priapism* is a condition where the penis remains erect for hours on end without stimulation or once the stimulation has ended. While that sounds like it would lead to a good time for all, it is a very serious medical condition, and it is often an indicator of other medical problems.

Priapus's connection to fascination, however, needs a bit more explanation. Like Fascinus, Priapus protects against the evil eye, and he does it in much the same way. While Fascinus wards off the evil eye through his presence in the form of a winged phallus, Priapus merely lifts his robes and displays his massive manhood. They never explain how either Priapus or Fascinus succeed against the evil eye in this way, but one theory is that they are so filled with life and vitality that ill-will cannot thrive in their presence. In some of my crasser moments, I joke that they might hold the curse at bay by dickmatizing the damn thing!

Perhaps the most famous phallic deity in any culture, bar none, is the Hindu God Shiva. Like Fascinus, Shiva can be represented abstractly through a particular type of stone called the *Shiva Lingam*, which is purported to intensify vitality, increase pranic energy levels, and bestow good health. (Side note: the Shiva Lingam can be used to represent any phallic deity.)

Within the *Linga Purana*, a sacred Hindu text, we find out that "The distinctive sign by which one can recognize the nature of something is therefore called a lingam" (*Linga Purana*, 1.6.106). Since newborn baby boys are distinguished from newborn girls by their distinctive sex organs, the penis became identified colloquially with the lingam. Shiva has many guises (paths or aspects), but in all of them he demonstrates some version of fascination. Ecstasy is the version of fascination most commonly associated with Shiva. His worship parallels that of Dionysus in its ecstatic frenzy and joy. As a witch, however, my favorite expression of Shiva's wild, ecstatic nature comes from his path as Pashupati, the Lord of Animals. In this path, Shiva strongly resembles the image of Cernunnos that so many modern witches hold near and dear to our hearts.

In fact, there is some cause to believe that they might be the same spirit. Most of the arguments that say that Cernunnos and Pashupati are the same spirit stem from analysis of archeological artifacts, specifically the *Gundestrup Cauldron* and the *Pashupati Seals*. It's a fascinating study, and I encourage you to research it further if you have a genuine interest in adding the Male Mysteries to your current magical practice as a witch.

In Norse mythology, this role is filled by Freyr, a phallic fertility god who belongs to the Vanir pantheon. His name means "Lord," and, in truth, this may actually be more of a title hiding the harvest god's true name. In her book *Taking Up the Runes*, Diana Paxson suggests that his name might be Ing, and she gives some pretty convincing arguments for her claim.

Like Freyr, Fergus from the Celtic pantheon, has numerous phallic connections. Some sources claim that his name actually means *virility*. One thing is certain from his mythology, though: he is the pinnacle of what it means to be male by any standard. He is viewed to be the perfect image of male beauty: a chiseled jaw, blonde hair, blue eyes, V-shaped torso, you get the idea. His manhood is described as being enormous. Some accounts claim that 7 fists can fit inside his penis.

Fergus's connection to fascination is best seen in his sexual relationship with the Goddess of Intoxication and the Sovereignty of the Land, Maeve. Maeve is said to have an even more insatiable desire for sex than Fergus. 30 men fail to exhaust her. So, if Fergus can hold Maeve's attentions, his ability to fascinate seems unquestionable, at least to me.

Various cultures throughout the world have similar mythic concepts of ithyphallic deities, who have dominion over the forces of production. This connection between the phallus and creation of the manifest universe can take the form of fertility, shamanic wisdom, even creation and destruction.

Whether we're talking about illusion (like the Hindu concept of Maya) or our Ancestors dreaming the manifest world into existence (like the Aboriginal Australian concept of the Dreamtime), we are dealing with the Order of the Masculine, since this manifest, produced universe of form belongs to the Masculine Order. It is up to the Order of the Feminine to undo all that has been done, to dissolve the fine distinctions of the Masculine, ultimately, to do away with the Masculine. The Divine Feminine does this by reabsorbing the Divine Masculine into Herself, taking us out of the manifest universe and back to our rightful place within the Godhead; doing away with all polarity in the process.

As long as there is a manifest universe, we are bound by the Law of Polarity, because the manifest universe is necessarily of the Order of the Masculine. The Masculine cannot exist without the "superhuman effort" of separating from the Feminine by creating distinctions, creating polarity.

This process of production, whether it displays itself as fertility, creativity, or whatever other label you wish to ascribe to it, has time and again been linked to the Order of the Masculine by various and independent cultures throughout the world. It makes no difference whether you wish to talk about this concept as fertility (either in the form of reproduction or as the light source initiating the growing cycles of the earth) or you want to talk about it as a liminal point in time where something or someone comes into being. The result is the same. These concepts have been linked to the Masculine Polarity for a reason, and those of us who wish to explore the Male Mysteries must seek to understand that reason on a deeper level for ourselves. This book only seeks to start you on that journey.

5 THE MAGICAL DYNAMO

Just as the Female Mysteries take the inherent power of the embodied female experience for women and use it to create a deeper understanding of occult or metaphysical concepts linked to that female experience, the Male Mysteries do the same thing for men. While it is very easy for some people to see the mysteries of the female biology, those same people often lack the eyes to see the corresponding mysteries of the male. That does not mean that there aren't any there to see. It only means that the Male Mysteries have been so well-hidden that people overlook them. Admittedly, the Male Mysteries are not common, even among male witches. I think one of the reasons for this is because they are so controversial.

Although they embrace the beauty in being male, the Male Mysteries do not glorify the masculine, and anything that does not worship at the altar of masculinity has a tendency to be repressed within our society. The Male Mysteries necessarily exclude women (as well as various other members of society who do not self-identify as *male*), and, if they are going to be performed to their fullest extent, the Male Mysteries require that initiates embrace homosexuality within themselves. All this is very controversial, and I can understand why it would have remained so well-hidden for so long.

On a purely biological level, the Male Mysteries begin to take shape with the production of sperm. According to Dr. Charles Lindemann of Oakland University, the average human male will produce roughly 280 million sperm cells in one ejaculate. In each milliliter of semen, there is roughly 100 million sperm cells, and the average human male produces between 2 and 5 milliliters of semen each time he ejaculates.[13]

Talking from a perspective exclusively concerned with potential output, semen is an incredibly powerful substance. In my opinion, its magical and energetic value is on par with women's menstrual blood, and it holds just as many secrets for the magical practitioner to uncover.

---

[13] Popiolek, Kim. "Dr. Lindemann's Fun Sperm Facts!" Dr. Charles Lindemann's Lab: Sperm Facts, www2.oakland.edu/biology/lindemann/spermfacts.htm.

Biologically, the potential inherent in any particular human male ejaculation (without medical intervention, of course) is one. On rare occasions two or more offspring may be possible. Even with the optimal conditions available and modern medical intervention, the largest multiple births from a single human coupling to date is recorded at eight babies. Though that seems like a relatively small output when considered as a fraction of the potential, think about how much that fraction can actually do.

What we're really discussing here is one future person added to the world. We're talking about one future will, directing his or her energy to influence the external world. What if that person was similar to Nelson Mandela, Albert Einstein, Rosa Parks, or Mother Teresa? What good could he or she do? What about the potential for harm if that person kept company with people like Countess Elizabeth Bathory, H. H. Holmes, Josef Mengele, or Jeffrey Dahmer?

Look at how each of these people changed the world for better or for worse. That only skims the surface of the discussion, but even that cursory investigation lets you glimpse the potential scope we're talking about here.

In either case, we are only discussing the power output of 1/280 millionth of what male semen can potentially produce. Imagine a possible world where the full potential power of this substance could actually be tapped. In this hypothetical situation, each individual man would have an entire population within him at any given moment. He would have the power of a nation behind his every whim and intent.

In 2016, there were 323 million people in the United States. We're only talking about a difference of 43 million people here (roughly the population of California). Imagine the energetic potential inherent in that concept! Have you ever been to a concert filled with a crowd of other people, focusing their attention on a performer? Have you ever felt the "electricity" their combined wills create? If you have, then you can begin to fathom the awesome power we're discussing here. That awesome power is available to each male witch who knows how to use it.

Even if you argue against my hypothesis of the united will of a crowd in each ejaculation, which is certainly your right, you still have to grapple with the awesome potential of even one single, solitary individual. Nobody on earth could argue that, as far as potentiality goes, it is reasonable to assume that semen's energetic value is at least equal to the production of one life. That unarguable fact alone gives us the very basis for a more in-depth metaphysical discussion on the Male Mysteries and how to tap them.

Whereas the Female Mysteries talk of blood and bone, the Male Mysteries talk about possibility and potential. Women may bring forth life and nurture it once it arrives, but it is the male who initiates the process and unlocks the potential of our human bodies to do what they do. Like the crossroads spirits who open the way, men are the gate keepers to these possibilities, and our role, as keepers of the keys, goes so much further than just being a "sperm donor."

There are real mysteries to be explored with regards to men and their role as keepers of potential. For some men (mostly Straight and Bisexual men), these mysteries might be explored through their role in the reproductive process. Other men find themselves exploring the Male Mysteries outside of human reproduction. Instead of focusing on producing babies, these men explore their power for potential in the realms of thought, art, and magic. Historically, these men have been what we, today, would call exclusively Gay men.

Our ancestors knew the value of Gay men to their communities, and, now, modern science is beginning to back up their wisdom. Even Freud recognized a powerful homosexual inclination in **most** adolescents. Regardless of the presence of heterosexual options, most boys and girls experience an association between their own biological sex and whatever they find sexual. Boys, especially, start out their sexual explorations by being fascinated by male genitalia (their own and others'). These early explorations often lead to orgasm and an association between male bodies and pleasure. For some children, this "immature homosexual response" disappears after the onset of puberty when they transfer their sexual desires to members of the opposite sex, but for others, it does not. This discrepancy was the foundation for much of the psychological bias about homosexuality being a stunted state of development throughout the 20th Century.

However, this philosophical stance merely shows us our own bias. Within various indigenous tribal cultures, these adolescent homosexual encounters provide young boys with companionship, which can help ground them during turbulent points in their development. These peer relationships help both partners learn about the emotional aspects of sex and bonding without risking pregnancy. In some cases, these relationships help young boys embrace a healthier sense of masculinity.

Within Western society, where homosexuality is stigmatized, most adolescents repress their "latent homosexual responsiveness," which only leads to insecurity about themselves and their "unnatural" desires, discontent, and, in some very extreme cases, suicidal thoughts.

Indigenous cultures did not suffer the disease of homophobia. In fact, Gilbert H. Herdt, a professor of human sexuality studies and anthropology who has taught at Stanford University, the University of Chicago, the University of Amsterdam, and the University of Washington, points out that among the Samba tribe of New Guinea, some males showed a strong drive towards heterosexuality, which corresponded to their declining interest in homosexual initiatory practices. Conversely, he says, some males continued frequent homosexual encounters long after their marriages had commenced. Herdt estimated that the total number of strongly heterosexual or strongly homosexual males amounted to roughly 5% of the tribe's population. The other 90% of males within the tribe demonstrated various degrees of bisexuality.[14] There is no reason for us to assume that, if Western culture relinquished its absurd hold on its own homophobia that we wouldn't have similar numbers.

Herdt's estimation about the Samba tribe matches my own hypothesis that most people within society would be Bisexual to varying degree with a much smaller (and equal) percentage of people who identify as exclusively heterosexual and exclusively homosexual as outliers. If we are correct, then nearly as much as 95% of the world's population experiences varying degrees of Bisexuality. Since we believe we already know so much about heterosexuality, shouldn't we also endeavor to understand homosexuality and get a better handle on the actual sexuality of 95% of the world's population?

Recently, scientists have begun to discover indicators that homosexuality might be a genetically inherited trait. Francis Mondimore tells us that Dr. Dean Hammer of the National Institute of Health examined DNA markers on the X chromosomes of family members. In the case of homosexual members of these families, Hammer found "certain markers" present on the X chromosomes, which were not present on the X chromosomes of heterosexual family members.[15]

---

[14] Herdt, Gilbert H. *Guardians of the Flutes*. Chicago: University of Chicago Press, 1981.
[15] Mondimore, Francis Mark. *A Natural History of Homosexuality*. Baltimore: Johns Hopkins University Press.

Physiological research of the brain has shown notable structural and functional differences in the brains of homosexual and heterosexual men. According to James Neill, studies have shown that the corpus callosum and the anterior commissure (bundles of fibers that connect the two halves of the brain) are larger in Gay men than they are in Straight men, which, ultimately, accounts for "greater functional symmetry."[16] Ultimately, this means that brain function is more evenly divided between the two hemispheres of the brain in Gay men than it is in Straight men. While Straight men tend to be better with things like eye-hand coordination, spatial relations, and other "right brain" activities, Gay men are better suited to balancing the polarities within themselves. Studies have consistently shown that Gay men can more easily tap the "left brain" functions (generally attributed to women) than their Straight counterparts.

The real value of this physiological discovery comes when we leave the realm of science proper and venture into metaphysics and occult philosophy. Gavin and Yvonne Frost studied the magnetic field surrounding living organisms for more than 20 years. Dr. Loy Stone (who was president of the Church of Wicca in the 1980s) performed experiments with a galvanometer on the magnetic fields of various participants. The Frosts tell us that through these experiments, they discovered that most men would deflect the galvanometer one way, while most women would deflect it the other.[17]

The most interesting piece of this story from *The Witch's Magical Handbook* (for me at least) is the words "most men" and "most women." Since a galvanometer can only go one of two directions, presumably some of those men deflected the galvanometer in the same direction as the women did, and some of those women deflected it more in line with the bulk of the men. Arguably, those anomalies might very well have been Gay men and Lesbian women. Unfortunately, we cannot know for certain, because that information wasn't published in the book.

On a biological level, most Gay men share a predominance for "left brain" functionality with women. On average, we tend to be drawn to the arts, to be caregivers, and to be adept at fine and complex motor skills, requiring delicacy (needlepoint, knitting, surgery). So, it is not a

---

[16] Neill, James. *The Origins and Role of Same-Sex Relations in Human Societies.* Jefferson, NC: McFarland & Company, Inc., Publishers, 2009, 70.
[17] Frost, Gavin and Yvonne. *The Witch's Magical Handbook.* Reward Books, 2000.

far cry to hypothesize that this shared mental functionality also makes Gay men and women energetically similar on a magical level, especially when anthropological research on indigenous tribal cultures the world over supports that theory.

Let me propose a theory. It is only a theory, but it is worth considering, since we don't have any other explanation for such pervasive historical facts regarding homosexuality.

Our ancestors operated on an intuitive wisdom that our modern sciences (including our occult sciences) are only now beginning to tackle realistically. Gay men (or men who were considered "gender non-conforming" in some other way) were the preferred magical workers of the ancient world. To be fair, our sciences are only addressing elements of this issue now because pervasive Judeo-Christian prejudices have halted the research up to this point.

If valid (admittedly this is a self-indulgent theory[18]), this theory would explain a great deal of the aversion to allowing Gay men to practice within some of the more traditional old guard covens. For example, Gay men might have interfered with the well-running of their group, but not for the reasons traditionally given to many Seekers who were turned away in the past. It's not that Gay men can't work magic within the structure of these traditional covens. It's more likely that their covens simply weren't set up to handle the unknowable effects of having Gay male witches within their circles.

I am not looking to point the finger of blame here. The traditional old guard covens did the best that they could with the information they had. Most of them were formed at a time when absolutely everything was viewed through the heterosexual lens. Even science is only now beginning to look at the biological differences inherent in sex and gender. How can anyone fault the old guard for going with what was proven to work?

But I digress …

On an energetic level, the functional symmetry of Gay men's brains might account for a great deal of the power that our ancestors attributed to Gay men. Why our ancestors viewed Gay men so favorably is still a question for debate; that they did view Gay men this way, is not. To better understand this dynamic, we need to dive a little

---

[18] The mere fact that it is self-indulgent doesn't necessarily make it wrong. If nothing else, even if it is wrong, I think it is worth exploring the connections this theory forces us to look at as witches.

deeper into old school occult anatomy.

Within the Western Occult Tradition, the male genitals were viewed to be primarily electric (energetically positive). Conversely, the female genitals were viewed to be primarily magnetic (energetically negative). Here's where it gets interesting, though: in both men and women, the anus was said to be primarily magnetic.

The anus being universally magnetic means that women would have two magnetic currents in their root chakra area, two negative poles. The root chakra area of straight or traditionally "masculine" men would still have a positive and negative pole, but not taking pleasure from engaging the receptive nature of the anus shuts down the potential power before it can rise. That's not to say that either straight men or women can't produce power on their own. Their own internal polarity still works to help them raise power. However, they gain a duplicating benefit from a partner's opposite polarity.

However, having a fully functional battery within the root chakra area and another fully functional battery within the head means that, in general, a Gay man can individually generate roughly the same amount of power as a traditional heterosexual pairing. The larger corpus callosum and the anterior commissure of Gay men essentially joins together two opposite currents in the head, like lining up the positive and negative poles of batteries in series. By engaging the magnetic (or negative) quality of the anus in a sexually arousing way, Gay men create a second battery within their bodies. This effectively makes each individual Gay man his own working pair. Therefore, two Gay men working together in a sexual capacity would effectively create a dynamo!

I propose this theory for one reason. I want to empower Gay men. In order to do that, Gay men need to have a sense of purpose, we need to find value in ourselves and within society. Personal opinion: to do that, we need to reconnect with our magical and spiritual gifts.

I do not propose this theory to create monster egos in Gay men, though I am aware that the potential is there with this theory. This dynamic potential that I have been talking about is actually a double-edge sword. It can harm us just as much as it can empower us. In fact, in many ways, without proper direction, it has already harmed us. The stereotypical drama, the overindulgence, and the hyper-focus on sex and addictive behavior patterns, which have been characteristic of the Gay Community in recent history—all stem from this unrestrained and undirected energetic potential.

Gay men have also been harmed energetically in another very real way. Our relationships are stereotypically short-lived. Have you ever heard that joke: "What's a gay second date?" Answer: "What's a second date!" It would be funny if it wasn't also so sad.

Earlier in this book, I talked about Bardon's take on the occult philosophy regarding the magnetic and electric fluids (or currents). Remember that they are opposites. While the magnetic is cold, the electric is hot. Whereas the electric is active, the magnetic is passive. So on and so forth.

Though Gay men are remarkably balanced energetically (as this chapter has professed), though our brains are more symmetrical in their development, and though our bodies create dual closed circuits, we cannot disregard the fact that this miraculous energetic feat is happening within the confines of the male body. The bodies themselves tip the scale towards the electric polarity, and that must be taken into account.

Remember, the electric pushes away, whereas the magnetic attracts. Because Gay relationships have two male bodies that are creating fields, which are somewhere between just slightly more electric to decidedly more electric, and because Gay men have not been adequately trained about how to balance out these energies within themselves, they wind up "pushing each other away," like two magnets whose North poles align.

The opposite is true for Lesbians. The rest of that sick joke, which I mentioned above, is: "What's a Lesbian second date?" Answer: "A U-Haul and cats!" No matter how balanced a Lesbian woman's energetic currents are, she cannot fail to take into account the effects of her body's magnetic pull. The female bodies of both partners tip the scale in favor of "pulling them closer together."

While this may sound like a dream-come-true for many Gay men, it is no more valuable than the alternative we suffer. Ask any Lesbian you know. They will tell you that the Lesbian Community has their own version of drama to account for.

The only real and viable solution for dating within the Gay Community is to learn how energy works so that we can learn how to control it. Turning a blind eye to these realities in the past has landed us where we are currently, with many Gay men isolated and alone, with no recourse to fix their undesirable situations.

By embracing our potential as energy workers, shamans, and witches, Gay men can experience our value firsthand in a healthy way. Hopefully, by placing ourselves within the long and noble tradition of magical workers (whatever title you choose to label that practice with), we might be able to use the wisdom of our ancestors to craft successful, happy lives for ourselves in today's world.

6 GAY MYSTERIES

Once you dive deeper into the Male Mysteries, they become less approachable to the casual observer. As inclusive as the public face of Witchcraft can be, none of the Gendered Mysteries within it are, actually, inclusive. They are not meant to be. They couldn't do their work if they catered to everyone.

A group that makes it their primary goal to explore the Female Mysteries must, necessarily, exclude men on some level. If they didn't, they would waste their time trying to explain the color green to a man born blind who has never seen color and has no point of reference to even start the discussion. All their efforts would be wasted, trying in vain to find a common language to explain something that he simply does not have the experiences to comprehend. In the process, they would be derailed from their original goal, and the deeper mysteries of their tradition would never be scratched.

Even a mixed-gender coven that chooses to let its members explore the Mysteries associated with their respective genders must allow the women to go off separately and tend to their affairs, while the men do the same. That is, they must do this if they intend for the experience to be meaningful and transformative for those who participate.

The Female Mysteries will not (and, in truth, cannot) include men. Men do not have the appropriate lived-experience to embrace the deeper wisdom inherent in those Mysteries as more than an intellectual understanding. Try explaining the menstrual cycle to a man. Naturally, he can understand the process. With empathy and a little effort on his part, he can come to intellectual knowledge, but he will never truly understand what a woman experiences during her cycle unless he has to go through that process himself. Intellectual comprehension is a far cry from the wisdom required for adepthood within any of the Mysteries.

It is my opinion that the Male Mysteries necessarily involve homosexuality as a central theme. While it is certainly possible (even beneficial) for heterosexual men to participate in these Mysteries, very few men who identify as truly and completely Straight and who are committed to maintaining that Straight identity in today's society will have the ability to or, in all fairness, the desire to explore these Mysteries to the fullest extent.

When discussing the actual Male Mysteries, the concern over the Male (or Masculine) Polarity is not, in fact, the whole story. It's not simply enough that one identify as *male*. Male Mystery practitioners must learn to embrace the power and potential inherent in the embodied male state, but they must also learn how to mitigate the weaknesses of that same position. Baudrillard and the Aradia Myth did an excellent job demonstrating how a slight distraction can undo the Masculine.

There is a deeper and richer exploration of these Mysteries, which begins to unfold once a man embraces his erotic and/or romantic love for the physical body and the energetic current of other men. I refer to this aspect of the Male Mysteries as the Gay Mysteries to differentiate it from the parts of the Male Mysteries that are easily accessible to all men. Even if that interest is only ever fleeting (i.e., it doesn't define him or the whole of his sexuality), there must be a willingness in each man who explores the Mysteries at this level to embrace the love of other men on at least some level for the full effects of the Mysteries to take root in him. This deeper exploration changes the quality of the experience that a man who chooses to embrace the Male Mysteries from this perspective will encounter along his path to wisdom.

The necessity for embracing some amount of homosexuality for a man wishing to explore the Male Mysteries at this level cannot be overstated. Even Odin had to suffer the slur of being labeled *ergi* in order to embrace the true potential of his own shamanism. Some accounts say that he not only suffered the slur, but he actually engaged in the deed.

Ergi is the old Norse word for anything they deemed to be "unmanly," and it was often used as a slur against homosexual men. The actual meaning of the words *ergi* and *argr* have been much-debated over the centuries, but as Raven Kaldera points out in *Wightridden: Paths of Northern-Tradition Shamanism*, some of the conjectured meanings revolve around a lack of morality, others talk about the "sin" of being receptive during anal intercourse, and others talk about the use of magic.[19] Personally, I think it's interesting that the old Norse language linked receptivity during anal intercourse to sorcery, because it

---

[19] Kaldera, Raven. *Wightridden: Paths of Northern-Tradition Shamanism*. Asphodel Press, 2007.

continues to validate the innate link between Gay men and magic.

The central role of homosexuality within the Male Mysteries owes its near-universal prevalence to two ancient concepts. According to Neill, the first of these concepts finds its roots in Stone Age soil—a belief about the essence residing in the head and expressed through the ejaculation of semen through the phallus. The second concept, that *only a man can make another man*, was a natural conclusion drawn from the first, since how else would the power be administered without a phallus?[20]

This belief was nearly universal, and not entertained solely by "primitive" peoples. Both Greece and Rome had their versions of this belief as well. According to Plato, in his *Timaeus*, the psyche is a seed, which resides in the skull and the spinal "generative marrow," and it "breathes" through the genitals.

The Greeks believed that a young boy could acquire the virtues of a noble warrior (his *arete*) through sexual submission to the warrior. We have far fewer cases of Roman initiatory homosexuality available to us than we do regarding other Indo-European civilizations. There are, however, plenty of well-documented cases of Roman homosexuality within the social sphere. That being said, there are at least some accounts of homosexuality in Roman initiatory practices, and they are most often recorded in mythology surrounding the military.

The Roman historian Livy depicts Romulus and Remus in scenes typical of male initiation rites, which are highly similar to rites found in other Indo-European groups. According to legend, the sons of Mars were raised in the forest by a she-wolf. James Neill tells us that the historian David Greenberg has suggested that the she-wolf in this myth may have actually been a male initiator.[21] If that is true, it might give us a better glimpse into the initiatory homosexual practices of ancient Rome's warrior cult.

Both the Celtic and the Germanic warriors engaged in similar pederastic homosexual practices. The records are much clearer on this front. However, what is not clear is whether these practices were inspired by the philosophy that a warrior's virility (and his other virtues) were passed to a youth through sexual intercourse, although it

---

[20] Neill, James. *The Origins and Role of Same-Sex Relations in Human Societies*. Jefferson, NC: McFarland & Company, Inc., Publishers, 2009, 117.
[21] Neill, James. *The Origins and Role of Same-Sex Relations in Human Societies*. Jefferson, NC: McFarland & Company, Inc., Publishers, 2009, 188.

is probable. Given the similarities between the Celtic and Germanic warrior cults and similar institutions found among the Melanesian tribes, it seems highly unlikely that this otherwise seemingly universal philosophy would be the one glaring difference between these two isolated peoples.

As another example, the Sambia tribe of Papa New Guinea has a very specific process for turning a boy into a man, which could take anywhere from 10 to 15 years. When a boy is somewhere between the ages of 6 and 10 years old, he is isolated from women. Over the next decade or so, the young initiate provides fellatio to older bachelors, who copulate with him to "make him grow." This is a process that every warrior within their society goes through.

In fact, remarkably similar practices show up within early European cultures as well. Both the Taifali and the Heruli (Germanic tribes) placed young boys into similar homosexual relationships with older, more experienced warriors. For the Taifali, the young boys remained the receptive partner in these relationships until they became adults and succeeded in killing either a boar or a bear. The Heruli took the relationship a step further, labeling the boys with demeaning terms like *slave* or *servant*. In fact, the use of terms like these for the initiate were extremely common in nearly all the Germanic tribes.

Celtic society also had an elite warrior class, which they called the *fianna*. Generally, boys began their initiation into this band of brothers around the age of 14. Unfortunately, the references to Celtic homosexuality are not detailed enough to establish whether their practices were initiatory or not. Most scholars hold the belief that this type of pederastic relationship would most certainly have been a part of the fianna. Unlike the Greeks and Romans, the Celts did not have a common practice of keeping a written record. They viewed it to be unmanly to need to write things down. Most of what we know about the Celts comes from their Roman conquerors or from Christian translators, so it is not surprising that information on this topic might be a bit sparse, especially after the Christians got their hands on the material.

Within many warrior bands, young men gained entrance to membership through initiatory acts of ritualized homosexuality with older, initiated male warriors. Homosexual relationships of this sort also existed in Africa. For example, homosexuality was a central component of the military apprenticeship within the Azande tribe's warrior society. The Azande had dominion over a region in central Africa, which is now composed of the Central African Congo. Similar customs exist amongst the Batak of norther Sumatra, a tribe of former head-hunters. Homosexuality between adult bachelors and young men is universal within their tribe, not just for the warrior elite. Initiatory homosexuality was even prevalent within the Amazon basin tribal cultures.

Homosexuality within warrior societies was not limited exclusively to pederasty, however. In fact, there seems to be just as much evidence for "pair-bonded" homosexuality as there is for the hierarchical variety. Within Greek culture, the concept of pair-bonded male warriors was so commonplace that it became a central theme within a great deal of their mythology. Hercules, perhaps the pinnacle of masculinity (even today), had countless male lovers, which we have removed from his mythology to maintain the illusion of heteronormativity. According to Plutarch, it would be impossible to name all of his lovers. However, for a healthy dose of spite, I'll list a few of the more famous male lovers here. Among their ranks were such famous names as Jason (of Argonaut fame), Hylas, Adonis, and, prized above them all, Iolaus (who, by some accounts, was also his cousin). Achilles also had his lover Patroclus, whose death unleashed Achilles's legendary anger on Troy.

These myths held so much sway that even real life Greek warrior societies were inspired to embrace the ideals of pair-bonded homosexual love discussed within them. The most famous of these warrior societies being the Spartans, whom we all know from the stories of The 300—150 bonded pairs of warriors. The Spartan warriors held up the love between Apollo and Hyacinthus as an ideal for their warriors to embrace with each other.

This underlying philosophy of a man's power residing in the head, led to another interesting practice, which has a direct effect on the Male Mysteries: Head Hunting! The Western imagination has a tendency to paint head hunting tribes as base and savage, but that is not the case at all. Once again, this practice seems to be universal as far back as the Stone Age. Even cultures that we hold up as "civilized" today, have a history of head hunting.

The Indo-European tribes (and all the cultures descended from them) engaged in head hunting. To be clear, that includes a vast swathe of both Asia Minor and Europe. The Celts were fierce warriors who were feared because of this practice.

Far more than mere trophies, Celtic warriors would collect the heads of distinguished enemies, to gain otherworldly powers. For the Celts, the head represented the very essence of being. That essence could survive the death of the individual, and, therefore, in possessing someone's head, one could take ownership over that person's spirit or, at least, his power.

The process for taking advantage of an enemy's power involved cleaning out the skull, gilding it, and using it as a sacred drinking cup in various rituals. Celtic warriors with a less magical motivation, tended to adorn their houses with the skulls of their enemies. In some cases, they merely affixed the enemies head to a pike in their camp.

The Scythians, who were located in what is now modern-day Iran, engaged in similar customs. The Greek historian, Herodotus, says that the Scythians cut off their enemies' heads, and impaled them on pikes to guard the house. Like the Celts, the Scythians also crafted sacred cups out of their enemies' skulls so that they could consume the enemies' strength and power.

The underlying motivation for this practice was to impart the drinker with the strength and power of the skull's original owner. It was not meant to debase the victim. It was actually viewed as an honor of sorts. The defeated enemy was strong enough, noble enough, powerful enough that you earned the right to partake in his essence by defeating him.

As society evolved along "civilized" channels, the significance of drinking from a skull was transferred to a ritual cup. While witches have traditionally viewed the ritual cup (or chalice) to be feminine in nature, anyone pursuing the Male Mysteries, especially Gay male witches, will find that the chalice has masculine powers as well. The true power of the chalice is that, as a Gay male witch's tool, it is actually represents of our ability to wield the powers of both genders.

While the ties between the Male Mysteries and homosexuality are easiest to see in warrior societies, the evidence exists almost universally in nearly every other area of society as well. It can be seen in both advanced and primitive civilizations alike.

Homosexuality served an extremely important function in helping to maintain social harmony within a tribe or community. In some cases, like with the *kikuana* (also known as *aikane*) in Hawaii, there were specially designated roles for exclusively homosexual men to serve in this capacity. According to the diary of John Ledyard, as cited by D. Michael Quinn, homosexuality seems to be prevalent, if not universal, among the Hawaiian chiefs. Each chief had his own aikane, and these boys were treated with great dignity and respect by other members of the society. In some cases, these companions also served as emissaries and protégés to the chiefs themselves. One chief, King Kamehameha the Great, was a former aikane.

It is important not to "slut shame" these men by writing them off as simply being part of a ruler's harem. The aikane were not whores. First and foremost, they were not required to sleep only with the chief. Many of them had sexual relationships with men their own age. There are even records of aikane having relationships with each other. There were as many ways for an aikane to fulfill their function within Hawaiian tribal society as there were people willing to sleep with them. Their title describes concepts that are more familial or at least more familiar than most people get with someone they might label a *whore*. These boys were romantic, sexual, and intimate friends to the men they slept with.

Another point against slandering the aikane with our own Western sexual biases is the fact that they also were not limited to functioning exclusively within passive roles in their relationships with other men. Generally harems (even harems of men) tend to be filled with passive sexual partners who can be molded to their master's desires. The aikane were not effeminate men nor were they cross-dressers. These facts make them unique among men filling similar roles in other societies. Some aikane even had wives of their own, and, as we have already seen with King Kamehameha, some of them went on to claim real political and social power in their own right.

We have a tendency to think of the entire homosexual spiritual tradition as being composed of sexually receptive or effeminate men, embracing roles traditionally held for women within the particular society in question. In truth, the roles reserved for homosexual men throughout history have run the gamut. Regardless of how someone expresses his homosexuality, there is probably a culture who honored that expression in some way.

In many cultures, the roles for exclusively homosexual men were certainly closely tied to the roles of women within that society. In other cases, like with the aikane, the roles were unique and distinct. Among the Zapotec tribe of southern Mexico, homosexual behavior is a common occurrence between men of all ages. It was a common practice for men on hunting and fishing excursions to engage in homosexual relations with each other for many of the South American tribes. The Tapirape tribal hunting parties even took it a step further by bringing along other adult males (who were not part of the hunting or fishing activities) simply to serve the members of the party as receptive sexual partners.

The belief that a man's prized qualities could be passed onto the next generation, or that men could comfort each other in ways that women simply couldn't, also found a home within the realm of education—most notably in the institutions set up by the Greeks and Romans. While the Greeks certainly embraced initiatory homosexuality within their various warrior societies (most notably with the Doric city-state of Sparta), it is the educational homosexuality of classical Greece that continues to fascinate the Western imagination today. Unlike their militaristic neighbors in Sparta, the goal of education in Athens was the production of good citizens. These philosophical differences most certainly modified the approaches to male homosexuality within these two societies.

The Athenians took the ancient concepts of the phallic cults (that power resided in the head and was administered through the phallus), and they extrapolated out their own version of the theory. If they wanted to educate these young boys in the values, beliefs, and manners important to their society, then the best way to do so, in their theory, was to transmit the virtuous character of older, successful men to these young boys through sexual relationships.

Conventional theories by mainstream academic historians state that the homosexual relationships of classical Athens were temporary, one-sided, and exclusively educational relationships between older men and youths. Even more troubling (for me at least) is the fact that these historians believe that these boys didn't gain any pleasure from the experience, hinting that the Greek educational structure was akin to what we might contextualize as rape.

However, a broader study of Greek historical, literary, and artistic traditions presents a drastically different viewpoint. Some of these relationships are maintained throughout the entire lifetimes of the two lovers involved. Stories (both historical and fictional) abound of youths seducing older men. Plato has the famous account of Alcibiades seducing Socrates in *The Symposium*.

There is another false belief that Athenian teachers did not have anal sex with their young male students, that if and when they did have what we might classify as "sex," they did it "between the thighs." We have already seen how the Greeks believed that a man's desirable qualities could be transmitted to a youth through the administration of the older man's semen through anal intercourse. There is no viable, non-homophobic reason for us to assume that the Greeks would eliminate the intercourse component of this system, while still retaining the basic premise that justifies the intercourse in the first place.

While the homophobic denial of academia is annoying, the next misconception that we need to address is, to my mind, far more serious. More serious because many pedophiles and other sexual predators living and breathing today use the Greek archetype of homosexual love as a justification for their case. The basic argument is that the Greeks did not recognize an age of consent, and that if we (as a society) weren't so wrapped up in our Judeo-Christian morality, we wouldn't either. Nothing, however, could be further from the truth!

The Greeks actually did recognize an age of consent. Granted, the age cited was a bit young by our own standards, but there were, in fact, moral standards in place that everyone in society was expected to honor and uphold. Generally, boys were introduced into these educational homosexual relationships in their early teens (around puberty). The youngest age cited for educating a boy in this manner was 12.

It helps to put things in perspective by pointing out that the average age for a girl to be married in Greece at the time was also 12 years old. For the Greeks, a 12 or 13 year old was sexually mature. They considered the introduction of sex at that point to be a normal and healthy thing.

For those who would read this book and attempt to use the Greek model as a way to justify their own predatory desires, consider this: historical records do not back you up. While there were certainly some differences of opinion on the subject, the age at which a youth was generally considered the most attractive or desirable was somewhere in the later teens—roughly around the same ages where most societies place the age of consent today.

Beyond the homosexuality inherent within the Male Mysteries, which will discourage most genuinely Straight men, there is a very real need for an exclusively Gay male tradition to explore these Mysteries. As we have seen, throughout history, there has been a special, unique, and separate place in spiritual circles for men who exclusively love other men. One of the more interesting pieces of the Gay Mysteries is our ability to bring good luck to our lovers.

Ancient Babylonian religious texts have a lot to say on this subject. One entry reads, "If a man has intercourse with the hindquarters of his equal [another man], that man [the active partner] will be foremost among his brothers and colleagues." Another verse says, "If a man has [homosexual] intercourse with a cult prostitute, trouble will leave him." A third says, "If a man has intercourse with a male courtier for one whole year, the worry which plagued him will vanish."

The temple priests of ancient Mesopotamia were viewed to have magical powers. One text says that "if a man touches the head of an assinnu, he will conquer his enemy." Like the Mesopotamians, many of the Native American tribes believed that sex with a Two Spirit individual brought about good luck. The Cheyenne included *he man eh*, which is their word for Two Spirit, in every hunting party because of this belief. He man eh took care of the men (emotionally and sexually), healed their wounds, and set broken bones.

I have seen this particular magical good luck express itself in my own life on several occasions, but, to be fair, I only noticed it after no less than three of my ex-boyfriends became wildly successful in their respective industries. The first ex-boyfriend made his debut on *Project Runway* in 2004. The second sparkled on the 2006 season of the HGTV series *Design Star*. The third achieved a smaller measure of fame in the bridal industry, selling wedding gowns for more money than most people plop down to buy a house.

Gay men, like witchcraft, exist everywhere. Every culture had its concept of the witch (as we would understand the term today), regardless of what title that culture gave the role. Every culture had its Gay male traditions. Therefore, a Gay male tradition of Witchcraft will necessarily have to scour the earth to reclaim the Gay male magical and spiritual practices that have been stolen from modern Gay men.

While I, personally, feel that the concept of *cultural appropriation* is racist and xenophobic down to its very core (and just another way to keep people apart), I do believe that we need to treat individuals and different cultures with respect. That said, Gay men actually do exist everywhere. We are a part of all cultures, and because of the depth of our European ancestor's imperialistic arrogance, Western Society's war on women, and the thoroughness of the Christian religion's desire to spread its gospel, Gay men no longer have a single, complete heritage to embrace as our own any more. All that remains available to us is to cobble together bits and pieces from various sources into a new, cohesive structure that will serve the needs of modern Gay men who feel called to engage in it. However, because of the damage done to the Gay Community and Gay men by this history of hate, it is essential that we actually do cobble something workable together.

7 GAY MYTHOLOGY

It is generally agreed that myth serves five purposes, and, by taking a look at these purposes, I think you'll agree that reconnecting with Gay mythology is a perfect place to start our journey back to a healthy sense of self as modern Gay men. First, myth explains how things came to be. The Aradia Myth did this. It described the origin of the material world and how the cycles came into existence. Second, myth teaches lessons and values about how one ought to act. Third, myth unifies a group and helps them define their identity. Fourth, myth explains social and religious rituals, and, finally, at the very bottom of the list, it entertains.

In our modern society, we teach myth exclusively as entertainment, and we ridicule anyone who takes it seriously. It's okay to study myth in an academic context, as long as you know its proper place and you are able to forget about it once it's time to come back to the "real world." No matter what you do, though, you certainly shouldn't hold it on par with scripture. Heavens no!

This disregard for the value of mythology is not just ignorant; it's irresponsible. The modern Gay Community is a perfect example of what happens when a society forgets its own history and its own mythology. It operates on a completely materialistic level, devoid of magic or mystery, drowning itself in booze and numbing the pain of living a detached, meaningless life with copious amounts of drugs and sex.

The best remedy for this condition is to help that society remember, and in my humble opinion, mythology can do just that. Perhaps the most important function of mythology when it comes to healing the Gay Community (specifically) is the unifying piece that can help them define themselves. That is why I am providing a sampling of the various Gay male mythologies from around the world to get you started.[22]

---

[22] Should you wish to reproduce my research, an excellent place to start would be James Neill's book *The Origin and Role of Same-Sex Relations in Human Society* and *Cassell's Encyclopedia of Queer Myth, Symbol and Spirit: Gay, Lesbian, Bisexual, and Transgender Lore*.

While the Aradia Myth explains the Male Mysteries so clearly, it is insufficient on its own to explain the role of Gay men within these Mysteries. For that, we must turn to various other myths. Chief among them are the myths of Dionysus. As described earlier in this book, the Dionysus myths offer so much to Gay men who wish to explore the Gay Mysteries.

After Hera inflicted madness upon him, Dionysus wandered the world. He journeyed far and wide, including Egypt, Syria, and points further East. In his madness-driven wanderings, Dionysus wound up in Cybele's cave, where the Great Mountain Mother restored his sanity. There he was, purified and made whole again, and he was taught the mysteries of the Great Mother. Dionysus, like the blacksmith mentioned earlier, was empowered by contact with the Earth Mother. In both cases, initiation into the magical arts is derived from proximity to her.

Cybele's intersexed birth gave her access to a power greater than any of the other gods. In fact, that is the reason that the gods castrated her when she went by the name *Agdistis*. Like the Native Americans, with their Two Spirits, the Greeks recognized the power of someone who could straddle the genders so completely. Cybele's access to the truth of the Primordial Feminine (as opposed to the socially acceptable "feminine") is the reason she could undo Hera's curse. No other goddess could have accomplished so much!

This myth reveals so much more than just the role of Gay men within the Mysteries (Male or Female). It plays with the construct of gender in a way rarely seen in myths that have survived into the modern era. Though biologically male, Dionysus is not the masculine force within this story. Hera is! Dionysus is as indistinct, in his own way, as Cybele.

While Cybele's fluidity happens on the physical level, Dionysus's own indistinctness is emotional and mental. He functions magically like a Gay man. Cybele functions like a Transgender person. They are each other's mirrors, presenting the opposite as a reflection of the real to each other.

Cybele is the archetypal Feminine that, according to Baudrillard, is indistinctness of gender. Hera represents woman as man would have her be. She is a projection of his ego—a wife, a mother, and a queen. She is content to rule under him and to seek her status through his glory. Give her a measure of power to ensure that she doesn't cause real trouble. Give her independence within your parameters so that she feels validated and doesn't threaten your own power base.

Cybele, however, is the wild card. She can't be pinned down, and she won't be controlled. She is the Feminine that actually stands opposite Hera as Masculine in this story. Dionysus is somewhere between them, and this reveals a truth about the Gay Mysteries within the Male Mysteries for anyone who has the eyes to see it.

There is another myth within the Greek canon, which reveals the role of Gay men within the Mysteries, and, like the Cybele Myth, it reflects in mythic language what our historical accounts have relayed academically. We are all familiar with the myth about Dionysus searching for his mother, Semele. Unfortunately, as is so often the case with Gay male mythology, the rainbow has been completely whitewashed out of this myth.

Dionysus searched far and wide for his mother. Sadly, she was nowhere on earth to be found. Eventually, he came upon Priapus, who claimed to have knowledge of her whereabouts. Dionysus struck a deal with Priapus: if Priapus told him where his mother was, they would have sex.

When Priapus disclosed her location, Dionysus pleaded with the phallic lord to postpone their intimacy to avoid leaving Semele in the Underworld for a moment longer than necessary. Priapus agreed, and Dionysus journeyed to the land of the dead to rescue his mother.

Once he had safely returned Semele to Mount Olympus, Dionysus set out to make good on his word. Unfortunately, Priapus had died by this point, so Dionysus found a fennel staff and topped it with a pine cone (some accounts say an artichoke). Then he stuck the wand in the grave right above Priapus's giant phallus, and he sat down on it. Due to its role in their love-making, that staff became the wand most associated with Dionysus (the Thyrsus).

This myth does some heavy lifting concerning the role of Gay men within the Male Mysteries. First and foremost, it reveals Dionysus as one of the premiere gods for Gay men. However, by detailing the god's journeys, this myth also gives us a clue as to our own purpose, which, as I have said, can be corroborated by historical accounts.

The most fascinating feature of this myth is that it shows the god willing to take the receptive role during a homosexual encounter, something tribal cultures attributed to Gay men who embrace the magical path. (Recall the Native American Two Spirit, Norse shamans, the Mahu of Polynesia discussed earlier.) Greek mythology is filled with Gay gods. Zeus, Apollo, and Hermes—they all have homosexual encounters, but, in each of those cases, it is the god who plays the active role and the mortal who is receptive to his lust. This mythological pattern harkens back to the universal belief that power resides in the head and can be administered through the phallus during anal sex. Ganymede, Hyacinthus, and Crocus (respectively) all received the essence of their divine lovers and benefited in some way from the association, becoming more like the gods they adored.

The fact that the Priapus Myth goes out of its way to detail Dionysus's sexual preference so blatantly is not merely creative license. It reveals something important. In every historical account of gender non-conforming men, it is the effeminate disposition and the willingness to be receptive during anal sex with another man that unlocks the power for the receptive man to fully embrace his own magical abilities. Portraying Dionysus as the receptive partner in conjunction with his Underworld journey seems to be hitting home a point that this book's anthropological journey through history has touched upon time and again: Gay men are meant to be the shamanic figure in their culture. For most of us who are of European decent, the shamanic figure in question is the witch!

Dionysus does not stand alone as the only male shamanic figure within the Greek pantheon to have sex with other men. In fact, there are plenty of other homosexually-inclined figures who take similar journeys. Unfortunately, most of their stories have been rewritten to take the homosexuality out of them.

According to some accounts, Orpheus was so distraught by his failure to retrieve his wife from the Underworld that he never took another female lover. It was Orpheus's interest in exclusive homosexuality and the jealousy of the countless women he spurned, according to Ovid, that lead to his ultimate demise at the famous Bacchic orgy.

Despite countless comparisons between Apollo and the rational or the forces of production, the Greek god of light was not without his ecstatic moments. As stated earlier, you will find a hint of the opposite in each pole whenever the Law of Polarity is in effect. It is no different with Apollo.

In his book *In The Dark Places of Wisdom*, Peter Kingsley reminds us of Apollo's ecstatic origins. He tells us that Apollo, like Dionysus, was a "god of ecstasy, trance, cataleptic states—of states that take you somewhere." He was shamanic!

In her *Encyclopedia of Spirits*, Judika Illes tells us that Apollo had more male lovers than female. In fact, he was probably the Greek deity with the most male lovers. Among his many lovers are Hyacinth (also spelled Hyacinthus), Carneus, Lapyx, and the god Hymen.

While journeying is certainly within the scope of Apollo's powers, his real shamanic talents tend to emerge with the arts of healing and prophecy. Both of these talents can be seen in his relationship with his lover Lapyx. Apollo wished to bestow the gift of prophecy on his lover, but wanting to prolong his father's life, Lapyx asked for the gift of healing instead.

Even Zeus, the King of the Gods, exemplifies the Gay male shamanic role, though he does so slightly differently. It rarely comes as a surprise that Zeus had at least one male lover. Most people know about Ganymede. However, his shamanic connection might be a bit surprising to even the most well-read scholar of myth.

As a shamanic figure, Zeus is most often connected to the Upperworld journey, instead of the Underworld, though he certainly has the ability to make that trek as well. This only seems fitting though, considering his title as *Sky Father*. The mythic key to unlocking Zeus's shamanic qualifications rests in his connection to the eagle.

In his book *Witchcraft and the Shamanic Tradition*, Kenneth Johnson tells us that the eagle serves as the totem for all shamans. He also tells us that it is the eagle, which sits atop the world tree, which the shaman uses to make his journeys. Mt. Olympus serves the same function within the Hellenic cosmology as the World Tree serves for various other cultures. They are both representations of the *Axis Mundi*. Zeus (in the guise of the eagle) sits atop Mt. Olympus. That's where he carried Ganymede in their famed flight.

In fact, Johnson claims that the eagle's connection to shamanism seems to be universal. He tells us that the Buryat have a legend that says that the gods sent the eagle to act as a shaman for humanity. The eagle then mated with a young woman, who slept beneath the World Tree, and their offspring was the first shaman. Many Native American tribes identify the eagle with shamanic qualities, because it flies the highest of all the birds. The heights this bird is able to achieve are supposed to be indicative of a purity of spirit.

Though I'm only focusing on it through the lens of Greek

mythology right now, the connection between men who love men and shamanism exists universally. While it is easier to see in tribal cultures, the connection between Gay men and magic exists in even the most "civilized" or "advanced" cultures.

Myth has so much more to teach modern Gay men than just re-exposing us to our spiritual gifts. History, anthropology, and sociology can do that. Myth alone can teach Gay men how to navigate the subconscious to undo the damage done by an overbearing heteronormative and patriarchal culture. Myth can help Gay men develop healthy, self-affirming identities, and it can help us better understand the nature of our relationships with each other, allowing us to find the love so many of us seek.

The love that Achilles had for Patroclus turned the tide in the Trojan War. Achilles, angered at being dishonored by Agamemnon withdrew his assistance from the Greeks, which was a huge handicap, but Patroclus, wanting to support his countrymen, convinced Achilles to allow him to marshal the Myrmidon army under Achilles's banner. Patroclus was killed by Hector during a confrontation with the Trojan forces and Achilles flew into a murderous rage at the news of his lover's death.

Plutarch wrote that Hercules had more male lovers than the god Apollo, an impressive feat since Illes claimed that Apollo had more male lovers than any other god. During the Twelve Labors, Hercules had Iolaos, one of his lovers, accompany him as his charioteer. Their love story was so passionate that it inspired real male lovers to pledge themselves to each other at Iolaos's tomb. Next in line for the title of his favorite was the boy who became his weapons bearer on Jason's quest for the golden fleece, Hylas. Among his many other lovers were such youths as Abderus, Admetus, Adonis, Corythus, Iphitus, who assisted in the hunt for the Calydonian Boar; Nireus, Nestor, another of Jason's argonauts (who eventually became King of Pylos). Even Jason, himself, was one of Hercules's lovers.

The oldest myth known to man is another "Herculean figure," whose homosexual relationship is central to his story. Like Hercules, Gilgamesh was a demigod, who had superhuman strength. However, the Mesopotamians were a bit less shy about his other "manly virtues." Book One of the Akkadian poem talks about how Gilgamesh raped the men and women, the daughters and sons of Uruk, the city where he was king.

Gilgamesh was indiscriminate in his choice of sexual partners. His appetites couldn't be satisfied, no matter how many people he "crushed" or "used." It was only after the town's people petitioned the Goddess, Gilgamesh's mother, for relief that Gilgamesh met his equal. Enkidu was a wild man from the wilderness. He was just as strong as Gilgamesh, and his appetites were equally insatiable. The pair-bonding between the two is a central theme of the story, which usually gets down-played by Western academia.

The most easily recognized case of homosexuality in Celtic myth exists between the famous shamanic warrior figure Cu Chulainn and his "foster brother," Ferdiad. Childhood friends, they wound up on opposites sides in a war. Cu Chulainn fought for Ulster and Ferdiad for Queen Maeve of Connacht. Cu Chulainn single-handedly held back Maeve's entire forces, nearly decimating her army until she sent the reluctant Ferdiad as her champion. Only pride sent Ferdiad to fight his love, and, for that pride, he lost his life, which devastated Cu Chulainn.

There are fewer cases of homosexuality cited within the Norse tradition, but there are still some tattered threads to pull at. Part of the problem with deciphering the Norse material is that most of it was written at least 200-300 years after the events, which are being described. In many cases the time lag was significantly longer. Some of the most famous Norse poems weren't written until the period between the 9th and 12th centuries C.E. Another part of the problem is that a great deal of the recorded material is delivered through the eyes of Christianity with its particular prejudices in full force.

However, there are some standard cases of homosexuality that are generally pointed to. Loki, the trickster god, is at least Bisexual. Odin's steed Sleipnir is a byproduct of one of his homosexual encounters. Odin, himself, is often accused of being *ergi* (or a passive homosexual) for his involvement in *Seidr*, which he learned from Freya.

Freyr, the Vanic god, was served by homosexual priests. This much, we know. Dumézil talks about a group of priests of Njörðr and Freyr who were honored, yet seem to have engaged in homosexuality as part of their spiritual role, like the Mesopotamian gala priests. These priests may have worn their hair in feminine styles or even dressed as women.

African mythology is as abundant on the topic of homosexuality as Norse is sparse. Talking about African myth as if it is one cohesive system, however, is a bit like talking about Native American myth or Asian myth that way. All three of these umbrellas cover large swathes of sometimes disparate peoples. No two Native American tribes operated in exactly the same way, nor did they believe exactly the same things. Japan is vastly different from China, which is vastly different from Korea. The same is true of the people in Africa. It is impossible to talk about an entire continent as one people, despite the neat, little box that our Western imperialistic imaginations have constructed.

I'm not exactly sure why this happens, but many people forget that Egypt is part of Africa. Whenever you hear the word *Kemetic*, it is most often associated with Egypt, because it is said to be the native label for Egypt. As one of the most well-documented civilizations in history, there is an abundance of LGBTQIA mythology available to us, although specifically Gay male myths are harder to come by.

When people examine Egyptian mythology for LGBTQIA themes, their minds immediately turn to the myth about Seth and Horus having sex with each other. In truth, most people identify Seth as Gay, because he is the "bad guy" of Egyptian myth, and our society loves to cast Gay men as the story's villain—Iago in *Othello*, Norman Bates in *Psycho*, and Scar in Disney's *The Lion King* are just a few examples. There are so many more LGBTQIA themes in Egyptian myth, however, that it is laughable that Seth is the sole character that springs immediately to mind.

By far, the biggest portion of these stories deal with beings we would identify as either intersexed or Transgender. Admittedly, as I have been saying all along, Transgender and Gay are not the same. However, because of the light that one will shine on the other (within the Egyptian context) and because most historical scholars had a tendency to talk about Transgender under the umbrella of homosexuality, I make an exception to include these tales here.

According to Sir Ernest Alfred Wallis Budge, in his book *The Gods of the Egyptians*, Ra was said to have a "double gender," with his female counterpart being Rat, who was said to be mother of the gods.[23] In hieroglyphics, Hapi, the god of the Nile, is depicted as intersexed. Though generally referred to as male, wearing a ceremonial beard, Hapi is simultaneously depicted with breasts. The god of the Mediterranean Sea, Wadj Wer, was often referred to as "the pregnant god." The pregnancy may have been indicative of his fertile nature, Wadj Wer

---

[23] Budge, E. A. Wallis. *The Gods of the Egyptians or Studies in Egyptian Mythology*. Chicago: The Open Court Publishing Company, 1904.

means "Great Green" after all. It may also be indicative of his gender fluidity as well. The god of fate was also intersexed, sometimes appearing as male, other times as female.

Even the Kemetic creator god, Atum, straddled gender. In one account, he masturbated into his own mouth and spat out his children. In another, he labeled his shadow as female and copulated with her to produce his offspring. In his book *Lifting the Spiritual Self-Esteem of the LGBT Community*, Khepra Ka-Re Amente Anu talks about how Atum was able to create other gods as a result of his "Bisexuality."[24] Anu goes on to say that Atum's gender was both male and female, which allowed him to impregnate himself, earning him the title "The Great He-She."[25] Atum, as an archetype, is certainly worth exploring for anyone who is working with the concept of polarity through a gender fluid lens.

Hindu mythology has countless examples of deities changing gender. Gods willingly change sex to engage in sexual intercourse with other beings at a whim. This prevalent gender variance does make it difficult to label any action taken by a particular god as *heterosexual* or *homosexual*, but there are also very real examples of undeniable homosexual encounters between specifically male deities.

While everyone is familiar with Shiva's bisexuality, there is another, lesser-known god, who has a better claim to homosexuality. While Agni, the god of fire, creativity, and wealth does have a wife in the mainstream stories, in other accounts, he is also married to the moon god, Soma. *Soma* is also the word used for semen in much of the Kundalini literature, which, combined with his marriage to the lunar deity, goes a long way to explaining Arthur Anthony Macdonell's translation of the Vedic verse that identifies Agni as "the best of Soma-drinkers."

There is a story about a sexual game that Agni and Shiva play together. In some accounts of this story, Agni provides fellatio to Shiva, while Shiva attempts to hold back his orgasm. In other accounts, Agni merely catches Shiva's *soma* in his hand and he drinks from there. In yet other translations, Shiva ejaculates into Agni's hand and Agni transports it to "the care-taker mothers" of Kartikeya. In some

---

[24] Personally, I find it odd that Anu would choose to use the term "Bisexual" to talk about what most people (in 2012) would have referred to as *Transgender*, but his point is still valid and should not detract from his overarching noble goal of elevating the LGBT Community.
[25] Anu, Khepra Ka-Re Amente. *Lifting the Spiritual Self-Esteem of the LGBT Community*. Bloomington, IN: iUniverse, Inc., 2012.

accounts, Kartikeya is the offspring of Shiva and Agni's game. This particular myth (in any of its interpretations) spawned the practice of throwing one's semen into the fire as a petition to the gods.

If accounts of Kartikeya's "womb-less birth" through Shiva and Agni's game are correct, than this elegant god of war and general of the demigods, would also qualify as a Gay god. The Gay and Lesbian Vaishnava Association claims that Kartikeya is traditionally worshipped as a bachelor who avoids women.

As a witch, who adores the moon, I find this next bit of Hindu mythology beautiful. Mitra and Varuna are emblematic of intimate friendship between men. In the *Brahmana*, these two gods are depicted as ruling over the waxing and waning phases of the moon. They engage in a homosexual relationship with each other and their lovemaking initiates the lunar cycle.

Next, we move on to east Asia, where Buddhism is the second largest spiritual tradition. While Buddhism, itself, does not generally distinguish between heterosexual and homosexual intercourse (both being seen as counter to spiritual growth), there is a plethora of instances where homosexuality is mentioned within Eastern mythology. In Japan, there is a folk belief that homosexuality was introduced into the world by Shinu No Hafuri and his lover, Ama No Hafuri, servants of a primordial goddess. The actual goddess whom they served is not universally agreed upon. In the Shinto religion, they have gods who, like the Greek Gods, engage in pederasty (referred to in texts as *Shudo*[26]). Shinto gods engage in all aspects of the devotees' lives. In Taoism, there is a spirit often referred to as *The Chinese Rabbit God*. He is not really a rabbit, however. *Rabbit* was a euphemism for *homosexual* in ancient China. This spirit was a man who ascended to godhood because of his love for another man. Because he was put to death for his forbidden love, Death, himself, elevated Hu Tianbao to godhood. As Tu Er Shen, Hu Tianbao is the Chinese deity who manages the love and sex between homosexual men.

Admittedly (and also unfortunately), my account of standard Western mythologies is a bit more robust than the other cultures reviewed in this chapter. On the one hand, that was unavoidable. There's just more information about the standard mythologies

---

[26] Outside of mythology, *shudo* was a samurai custom in which adult samurai engaged in pederastic relationships with younger boys.

available. On the other hand, that was also intentional.

I did my best to show that the Western mythic canon that witches traditionally pull our mythology from does, in fact, accept Gay men. However, because I genuinely believe that all cultures have their concept of the witch, just as all cultures have LGBTQIA people, I also wanted to open the possibility that a Gay male witch of Asian, African, Indian or any other cultural descent could find inspiration within the mythologies connected to his own heritage.

That said, since my personal heritage is mostly European, I didn't want to run the risk of following in my forefather's footsteps by trying to tell the stories of other cultures. I only wanted to point out that the same revelations, which exist for Gay men in European mythologies also exist in the myths of other cultures. Homosexuality is a universal human good, and every culture on earth has uplifting stories that account for its place within their cosmology. You may just have to dig to find it.

Hopefully, this chapter has sparked an interest in you to scour the mythologies connected to your own heritage and find personal validation within those stories. May the brief accounts of Gay heroes, gods, and spirits previewed within this chapter encourage you to enrich your own magical and spiritual practices with Gay-affirming materials. I genuinely hope that these stories will help you to find your own divine spark as a Gay male witch.

8 MAGICAL TRAINING

Most Witchcraft traditions have three grades of initiation. Some have a dedication period before the first grade. Others do not. Neither method is right or wrong. It's simply a matter of style. In Gala Witchcraft, we have chosen to include the prior dedication phase, because it is a small commitment that gives the Seeker a chance to determine if our tradition would be a good fit for him. The dedication phase also gives us a chance to see if the Seeker would be a good fit for us. It must be mutually beneficial.

You will find a dedication ritual in this book. It is not a dedication into Gala Witchcraft. We have our own private dedication ceremony for Gay and Bisexual men who want to explore the Gay Mysteries with us. If, after reading this book and doing these exercises, you decide that you might want to take the step towards initiating into Gala Witchcraft, we encourage you to reach out to us through the contact page at the back of this book. That said, the dedication in this book is a declaration of your desire as a Gay or Bisexual male witch to embrace the Gay Mysteries within the Male Mysteries as part of your own unique spirituality.

You'll notice that this section starts with a series of exercises. They are placed first within the text to make the dedication ritual more meaningful to you. They are standard exercises that most well-trained witches already know. I put them here for the Seeker who is new to his path.

I have put these exercises into my own words and added my own spin to them, offering bits of wisdom, which I have garnered over the years I spent training the witches in Gala Witchcraft. They are taken from a variety of sources. The first is my hypnosis training from *The National Guild of Hypnotists*. Theosophy (specifically Helena Blavatsky's work) was also a huge influence on this section. Franz Bardon's work in Hermetics was extremely helpful in providing structure and a great deal of content to flesh out the philosophies of the other two institutions. *Self-Initiation into the Golden Dawn Tradition* by the Ciceros was worth its weight in gold to me on this project, as was Raji Dorotez's *The Scarlet Wand*. Last, but certainly not least, were various

Hindu sacred texts.

If you have already done these exercises in one form or another and you know that you have the necessary talent to have a meaningful energetic and spiritual experience in the dedication ritual, you may feel free to skip ahead to the exercise of making your own bullroarer. It is the last exercise before the dedication ritual. As I've said, these are standard exercises for developing psychic talent, so if you have any doubt (or, conversely, if you attempted the dedication and it lacked meaning or power for you), I would encourage you to spend the necessary time developing the psychic talents listed in the beginning of this section.

Aside from developing your psychic talents, the exercises leading up to the dedication ritual are also meant to build patience, strengthen the will, and demonstrate your dedication to the gods. Be firm, even unyielding with yourself. Hold yourself accountable to the process, and, above all else, keep silent about your activities. Do not let other people's negativity harm your progress.

In addition to being firm with yourself, avoid criticizing others in any way during this phase of your development. It breeds negativity, and, eventually, the animosity that they feel towards you will rebound upon you. You don't need other people's negativity directed at you, making your job any harder.

Keep a journal for your work within the Gay Mysteries. Carefully record your successes and failures for all of these exercises in your magical journal. Make sure to include the days and times of your practice. Also include the duration of each exercise or ritual that you do. Take stock of astrological timing, the phase of the moon, day of the week, and any other information that you might want to remember when looking back on this process later. Magical people keep records. If you are thorough and diligent, then, later on, you will be glad that you wrote this stuff down.

MEDITATION

The power of the witch is the power of thought. I cannot tell you how many Seekers adamantly insist that they cannot meditate. They wear their laziness like a handicap that the world has to accommodate, never realizing that it is the height of foolishness to tell someone that you are a witch and, in the same breath, confess that you cannot or will not meditate. That would be a bit like a chef telling you he can't operate an oven, or simply that he refuses to. Meditation is the most basic skill a witch needs to master in order to develop his other magical talents.

More to the point, everyone can meditate. It's just a matter of persistence. If you refuse to develop this basic ability for yourself, give up now. The path of the witch is not for you.

If you still want to pursue the witch's path ...

1. Start by spending 5 minutes simply observing your thoughts. Don't try to stop them. Don't try to control them. Just observe them. Once you have achieved 5 minutes without breaking your focus, add a minute each day until you reach 10 minutes.
2. The next day, start over by attempting to hold just one thought. At first, you may find it exceedingly difficult to hold that single thought for any longer than a few seconds without letting other thoughts creep in on you. That's a great start! Be proud of yourself, but keep pushing through. Build up to a few moments. Hold that one thought, without letting any other thoughts intrude and without losing your focus, for 10 solid minutes. When you succeed at this endeavor, move on to the next exercise.
3. Eliminate all thought from your mind, and just be present in the NOW. You may only get a few fleeting seconds where your mind remains empty, a blank slate. That's ok. Start there. That's your baseline. Build up to 10 minutes by incrementally increasing your "stamina." Once this is accomplished, you can move on to the next exercise.

All told, this exercise could take anywhere between three weeks to about six months. Gently build your practice from a few moments a day to a solid half hour. Do it over time, and you'll see how easy it can be.

PERSONAL INVENTORY

This is very similar to the Fourth Step in Alcoholics Anonymous (AA). It's a personal inventory of all your strengths and weaknesses. AA refers to this exercise as "a searching and fearless moral inventory of ourselves," which, in truth, is incredibly witchy of them.

Most witches do a similar, smaller-scale inventory like this at least once a year within the seasonal cycles. However, it's a good idea to take stock at the beginning of your journey and transmute as many of your negative qualities to positive attributes as you can. At its core, this is an alchemical process.

Ultimately, this is an exercise in self-control. You must have the strength of will to look at yourself objectively, to see what is actually there, and not just what you want to see. Don't sugarcoat it. Don't make excuses. Don't pass a minor shortcoming off as irrelevant. Be merciless with yourself. Root out all your faults.

That said, *objectively* also means don't be unduly harsh with yourself, either. While you are taking stock of your shortcomings, you must also recognize your strengths, and your gifts, no matter how big or small. Catalogue them all. Don't exaggerate them. Don't minimize them. This is not the place for ego or false humility. It's a balancing act meant to teach you to see things as they really are. If you can see the truth about yourself, despite your fears and insecurities, you can see the truth anywhere.

The more you discover now, the better. Leave no stone unturned. Record all weaknesses and all strengths in their finest detail in your journal. Take one whole page and record your weaknesses there during the first week of this exercise. Do the same with your strengths. You can do one first and then the other or you can do them at the same time. It doesn't matter, as long as you are thorough in your discovery of both. Generally, this portion of this exercise will take most people about two solid weeks.

Once you have both lists laid out to your satisfaction, go back over them and ascribe an elemental quality to each trait—whether it be a shortcoming or a strength. For example, both a *quick temper* and *enthusiasm* would be labeled with an (F) for Fire. You might ascribe a (W) for Water to traits like *shyness* and *tenderness*. Do not stop until you have found an elemental label for each trait on both your lists. It may take you two more weeks, though I doubt it. Most people find that the ball really gets rolling by this point.

However long it takes you, be present in the moment. Don't rush to get ahead of yourself. You will be glad you took the time to slow down later on. Generally people tend to accomplish this exercise within three weeks to one month.

AUTOSUGGESTION

After you get your conscious thoughts under control, it is time to tackle the subconscious mind. The subconscious is the root of many of our current struggles in life, which is why it is often referred to as an *adversary* or is spoken about in antagonistic language.

Left untrained, the subconscious can wreak havoc on our lives. It is the seat of everything that is undesirable in our lives. For the Jewish people, this is the fabled Satan that we've all heard so much about. The Christians are the ones who turned Satan into a mythical being. Satan is not a being at all, breathing fire and brimstone. No matter what the Christians say, he is not Lucifer. In most translations of the Hebrew texts, the word *Satan* is usually translated as *Adversary* or *Opponent*. For the alcoholic, Satan is the desire to drink. For the reformed criminal, it is the desire to commit crime. Only the Christian faith removes responsibility for a person's actions by blaming it on the work of their mythological devil.

However powerful the subconscious might be, it does not work instantly. It requires both time and opportunity for its influence to manifest—for either good or ill. In order to transform the subconscious from a satanic force of chaos into a guardian angel that smooths the way for our successes, we must first learn to decode its symbolism, and we must remove the dimensions of time and space from its purview.

When I work with smoking cessation clients as a consulting hypnotist, we use the power of their subconscious to their benefit in this way. We work together to impress upon the client's subconscious mind a suggestion that something goes something like this: "I am a non-smoker."

We do not use an auto-suggestion like "Tomorrow, I will stop smoking," because it gives the subconscious ample time to wiggle around and place obstacles to success in the client's way. If you remove the elements of time and space by stating affirmations in the present tense as if they have already been accomplished, you transmute the subconscious mind's power for your own benefit.

Take a look at your list of shortcomings and begin crafting

affirmations in a positive tone, in the present tense as if they have already happened. For example, someone who struggles with a short temper might affirm, "I am calm and patient" or "I am happy" or "I am content"—whatever speaks to his own set of circumstances for why he actually has a short fuse.

Take charge of yourself. Write your affirmations to craft your balanced personality, attempting to balance out the elemental forces within yourself. If you have a preponderance of Fire energy, but you lack Earth, it might be wise to craft affirmations that will highlight the missing element. For example, that same person with the short fuse might affirm, "I am patient." We will use these affirmations in the pore breathing exercise, so craft them wisely.

This exercise can take up to two weeks. Generally, it goes faster if the witch is diligent about his work.

VISUALIZATION TRAINING

While you are crafting your auto-suggestions, gather together three or four everyday objects. (There's no reason that you can't run these exercises concurrently. It will save time.) Simple shapes are better to start with, but the items can be anything that call to you (a ball, a spoon, a vase, a pen, a phone). Study the first object. Turn it around in your hands. Review all its surfaces and its crevices. Be thorough in your observations. Then close your eyes and attempt to reproduce the object in your mind. Make the mental image three-dimensional. Turn it around in your mind's eye. You are going for an exact replica here. Do this with the other objects as well.

In the beginning, you may only be able to visualize the object for a few seconds. Some people may struggle to see anything at all. If you are one of those people who "can't see" (I was), you will have to work a bit harder, but perseverance will eventually pay off in time. Should the object disappear or your mind start to wander, center yourself and recall the object.

If you struggle with producing any image at all, start out by describing the object in words using your internal mental voice. Just concentrate your attention on the object in question. While you describe the object verbally to yourself, continue attempting to bring up a mental image that matches the description you are giving yourself, but do not beat yourself up if you never produce the image in your mind. Some people really struggle with this for a very long time.

Regardless of whether you can produce carbon copy replicas or you "visualize" in another way, you will know that you are ready to move on from this exercise when you can hold your attention on the object and really "sense" it in your mind in some way for a consecutive ten minutes without any interruption. Generally, this exercise can take between two weeks and six months to perfect. Ideally, the adept witch will return to this exercise again and again to hone his talents, raising them to new levels with each repetition. This is one of those exercises that you can use for the rest of your life.

PORE BREATHING

Your daily meditation practice should have become routine by this point, leaving you to deepen the techniques you use during your regular meditation. Pore breathing will allow you to better take advantage of this sacred time of quiet contemplation. For as effective as pore breathing is, it is also surprisingly easy to do.

During your meditation sessions, imagine that you are breathing not only with your lungs but breathing through every pore in your body. Engage your witchy imagination, and visualize your pores sucking in the vital force of the universe, like a vacuum. By this point, your meditation practice should be somewhere between 15 and 30 minutes. (If you're not currently at that point, begin incrementally working your way up to it.)

After you have attained a certain amount of skill with this activity, it is time to put the exercise to good use. In addition to your regular meditation, add another session. Don't stress. This second session will be brief. You can probably even do it while waiting at the doctor's office or during the length of a TV commercial (if you put the TV on mute).

Sit comfortably in a simple seated position with your legs crossed in front of you. Close your eyes, see your pores open up, while visualizing the vital energy of the universe being pulled into your very being, infusing every cell with that vitality. Now, mentally pick one of the shortcomings, which you have been working on (from your personal inventory).

1. Choose only one negative trait at a time, and focus on it for the full length of the session.
2. Use the corresponding affirmation you wrote to help you transmute that negative quality to a strength with another elemental association.
3. Visualize the element associated with the desired strength entering through your pores.

That's all you have to do in order to make real progress here.

Watch as the vitality of the universe begins to morph and turn into the desired element. Breathe it in through every pore of your body. Let that element fill you, and, as it does, repeat the affirmation silently to yourself in your mental voice. Hold the breath for just a moment, then exhale the old, undesirable quality (and element) out of your system, watching it transmute into the new elemental quality you have chosen for yourself.

Remember: your goal here is to balance out your elemental nature, so if your intuition tells you that you have been successful transmuting one quality into another, stop when you get the indicator and move on to the next quality, even if you still have more time left in your meditation practice that day.

This process can take quite a while for some people. For people who only have one or two negative qualities and a fair balance of the elements within themselves, it can take a week. For others, it can take months. Dedicate a solid month to practicing this exercise exclusively. After that, continue to transmute your shortcomings into strengths while you progress with becoming psychic.

BECOMING PSYCHIC

As above, so below. Our physical senses have their spiritual counterparts. Clairvoyance (also called *second sight* or *astral sight*), clairaudience (astral hearing), and clairsentience (psychic feeling) are the most commonly referenced. However, there are also spiritual senses of taste and smell, which can be used to good effect by a witch predisposed to engage those senses. (Since so few people actually rely on taste and smell psychically when starting out, I will avoid discussing their development here. We can save that for a future work.)

You will be naturally talented in one of the 3 main psychic talents. Your ability with the others may be marginal or even non-existent in the beginning. Do not let that stress you out. All three of these methods of retrieving psychic information can be learned by anyone who is clever enough and persistent enough to push past the initial stumbling blocks.

The information I give you here is a good starting point. It's traditional and time-tested. That said, for some of you, it may not be enough. Do not give up if that's the case for you. Use it as an opportunity to deepen your own spiritual and occult knowledge. There may be a very good reason that you have to struggle to learn this on the front end. Refrain from taking it personally, and, above all else, refrain from judging yourself. It will only make the obstacles more pronounced.

Clairvoyance:

Most books that seek to help the budding witch develop his powers of clairvoyance talk about gazing upon an object, like a crystal ball, a magic mirror, inky water, or some other reflective surface. To my mind, this is putting the cart before the horse. These tools are only useful after someone has developed the talent for clairvoyance. They do not help in its actual development.

Clairvoyants awaken their talent in a variety of ways. The first method only happens for a lucky few, who are born with it. They do not have to struggle to develop their talent. It has always just been there for them. My mentor in witchcraft has this particular blessing. While it is ideal, there is absolutely nothing any teacher can do to help this type of development. It either exists or it doesn't. Plain and simple. The second type of clairvoyance happens due to a traumatic experience, like an accident, a stroke, or some other type of shock to the person's system. Once again, a teacher will be useless in helping a Clairvoyant develop his talent through this method. The third is drugs, which work well but have their own dangers. Since those dangers are so great, no reputable teacher will advocate that you develop this talent through the use of drugs. The last method for developing clairvoyance, and the only one a teacher can help with, is practice and hard work.

That sounds like the same old platitudes you've heard all along, but we are not stopping at the platitude. I assure you. When I was a student in my mentor's coven, I would constantly ask him, "How did you do that?" Invariably, the response was, "You just do" or some other equally and infuriatingly vague answer. It frustrated me to no end, because I was fascinated by his talent, and the ease which he managed it made me feel weak and stunted by comparison. Today, as I look back on my education in the Craft, I am grateful for his vague answers (and his talent), because they forced me to search out the secrets for myself.

The element most associated with the eyes is Fire. Light is a manifestation of the Fire element, and it is light which allows the eye to do its work. We are going to take advantage of that scientific fact to help you develop your own clairvoyant potential.

Sit in a simple seated position with your legs crossed in front of you. Start by breathing in and out through the nose. Then imagine that you are breathing through every pore in your body. (See how these exercises build upon each other?) Imagine yourself surrounded by universal light. See it as being similar in nature to natural sunlight. Begin by seeing your body as an empty vessel, enveloped by this universal light. As you breathe in with every pore, see the empty vessel that is your body filling up with this light, like your cell phone battery icon recharges itself when you plug the phone into the wall. Now, with your internal mental voice, command the light to take on the attribute of clairvoyance. *"Light, you are now clairvoyance,"* or something like that. Tell the light that it sees everything. Tell it that neither space nor time present obstacles for it.

Continue this process until you are absolutely convinced that the light exists all around you and that it actually does possess the attributes that you have commanded. It may take a while at first. Don't rush it, but when you are absolutely convinced that this is so, move on to the next stage of the exercise.

Once you have completely filled yourself up with the light and you feel your body radiating with its power, imagine the light moving inward from your extremities (start with your feet and hands) towards your eyes. Condensing as much of this light-energy in your eyes as possible. Imagine your eyes glowing with clairvoyant light.

Now imagine your eyes possess all the attributes that you imbued in the light itself. Remain with this exercise for at least 10 minutes. If you have been consistent with your meditation practice up to this point, simply replace whatever former style meditation you were practicing with this exercise and kill two birds with one stone, so to speak.

When you are ready to close out your meditative practice for the day, imagine the light dissolving from your eyes. See it move out from your body, back into the universal source from which it came. Tell your eyes that they return to normal, and end your meditative practice. In time, you will be able to use this technique at will with a moment's notice, but in the beginning, you will need to practice each step exactly as it was given here in this section.

Should you struggle with this exercise or should it fail to produce results quickly for you (within a month), there is an additional tool which you can use to quicken your progress.

You can make a universal fluid condenser by boiling chamomile flowers in water. Let the herb roll around in the water for 3-5 minutes, then remove it from the heat and let sit covered. (Should you want to kick this up a notch for the purposes of developing clairvoyance, you can add eyebright to the mixture in a 2:1 ratio, favoring the chamomile.) Filter it and store in the fridge for up to a week or until it begins to mold.

Each night before you go to bed, soak cotton pads with this fluid and place them on your eyes for at least 10 minutes. As you soak the pads in the liquid, mentally tell yourself that you are developing your psychic sight. Construct an affirmation for yourself and repeat it over and over again, like a mantra if that helps you. Continue doing this for 3 more weeks. If you still have not achieved success, seek initiation into a reputable coven that can give you more advanced training.

Clairaudience:

The procedure for developing clairaudience is similar to that for clairvoyance, except the symbolism of the light and the eyes is replaced with the symbolism of the Akashic principle (also called *ether*) and the ears. (I believe that the old occult writers used Akasha or ether because it was easier to visualize than air, but I don't know that for certain.)

When you engage in your meditation practice over the next 3 weeks, you will be using your universal fluid condenser and two cotton wads formed to fit inside your ears. Moisten the cotton slightly with the universal fluid condenser (made just from the chamomile recipe above), and place them inside your ear cavity, like ear plugs. Imagine the Akasha principle (see it however it makes sense to you) collecting around your entire head. Once it has enveloped your whole head, see or imagine it moving into your ears, filling that space with its essence. Transfer your consciousness there, and breathe into it.

See your body fill with Air like a balloon, and feel yourself filling with the power of clairaudience, awakening the gift within you. After roughly ten minutes, deflate the balloon in your imagination, feel yourself becoming heavier and descending back towards the space occupied by your physical body, and release the Akashic principle through your exhalation. (I always giggle when I think about this. It reminds me of those old cartoons where the character blows smoke out of his ears.) Tell yourself that you are clairaudient, and watch the Akashic principle return to its universal source in its original form. Reaffirm for yourself that your hearing returns to normal. This is important, because we always want to be in control of the psychic information that we receive. We do not want to always leave the channels open.

Should you wish to turn on your clairaudience for a ritual or another exercise, all you need to do is call forth the Akashic principle with your imagination, see it moving into both of your ears, and allow it to open your psychic sense.

Clairsentience:

When you sit down to your daily meditation, begin using pore breathing to accumulate the Water element within your body. (If you have a fear of drowning, you can always sense Water purely as Coldness and eliminate the negative stimuli. The benefits will be the same.)

When you have filled your body with the element of Water, load the Water inside you with clairsentience through the power of your witchy imagination. Do not move on from this point until you are completely convinced that your wish is strong enough to awaken this ability within your astral body.

Project the Water element out of your body onto a piece of flannel, linen, or cotton, which was already moistened with the universal fluid condenser made from chamomile alone. You must make sure to release all of the Water element from your body. We will not be using the Water element directly in this exercise, only its magnetic properties. Focus on projecting the Water from your solar plexus chakra, the center of gut reaction.

Lay flat on your back for this meditation. You can use the floor, couch, or bed. Raise your head slightly. You should be comfortable, like you are when you get ready for sleep each night. No matter what happens, though, you must avoid actually falling asleep. This exercise is so relaxing that the potential for drifting off is very real. Should that happen one time, resolve to not let it happen again. Do not build a pattern of falling asleep while meditating!

Place the cloth moistened with the fluid condenser and the Water element on your solar plexus. Close your eyes. Now imagine yourself floating peacefully in Water. You are light and buoyant, and you have no problem breathing normally as you float.

Once you are peacefully floating on your imaginative Water (or a field of buoyant coldness, if you prefer), transfer your consciousness to your solar plexus. Think about how the Water around you and within you acts as a magnetic force, attracting astral clairsentience to you. You must be able to imagine the magnetic attraction so thoroughly that you actually feel its pressure in your solar plexus, like two magnets pulling towards each other in real life.

When you are ready to end this meditation session, see the Water evaporate into nothingness, returning to its normal state within the cosmic order. At the same time, you return to your normal state of awareness, slowly and peacefully. Remove the cloth, open your eyes.

Whenever you wish to call upon this power within yourself, shift your consciousness to your center of sentience (your solar plexus). That is all that will be required once you have perfected this exercise. Like the other two senses, it may take some time. If it does, be patient.

It will come.

Generally perfecting all three exercises can take anywhere from nine weeks to a whole year.

MAKING A BULLROARER

Until the middle of the twentieth century, nearly 10 to 20 percent of the cultures in the South Pacific practiced male homosexuality within a ritual context. The numbers were much higher before Western patriarchy and Christian missionaries spread their influence. Today, those numbers have dwindled even lower.

In a region of Western New Guinea called Papua, there is a tribe called the Marind-anim, which is famous for one of its rites of passage. The rite is called the *Sosum* Ritual. The word *Sosum* translates as *Bullroarer*.

The Sosum Ritual is a central piece of male initiation within that culture. During the ritual, a central phallus is erected, and everyone dances around this central point. The phallus is said to honor an ancestor whose mother-in-law castrated him while he was copulating with his wife. After the dancing, the previously initiated members of the society entice the newly initiated into homosexual intercourse. Academic scholars hypothesize that the events of the Sosum Ritual stem from the belief that vaginal sex will pollute the male body and, ultimately, end in death.

Within Pacific Island cultures, the bullroarer symbolizes masculinity. In general, it is shaped like a flat, pointed oval. It's constructed out of wood, and painted red, white, and black. Some are covered with geometric shapes or other organic patterns. A hole is drilled in one end to accommodate a cord. Men use the cord to whirl the bullroarer over their heads so that it spins on its own axis. The characteristic sound (or roar) that it makes can be heard from miles away. Some people argue that the bullroarer emits the voice of the spirits. Others say it was used as a method of long-distance communication between the men of the tribe.

Let me address the Politically Correct Contingent again, regarding the topic of cultural appropriation. I believe that the use of the bullroarer in a new context (as we will use it here) is not cultural appropriation. I feel this way for a few reasons.

First, I view our use of this tool to be open-minded inspiration that recognizes the value of another culture's wisdom when our own culture fails us so miserably in establishing something comparable. While our context honors the spirit of the original ritual, we are not attempting to steal the actual content of the ritual, itself. Our use of this tool has been modified to fit a modern magical practice, while still maintaining the original intention of the tool.

Second, the morphic resonance of this tool is not only connected to the tribal culture where it was created. It is also connected to homosexuality and men loving men, which is universal.

Third, while there are still Marind-anim (or Marind) people alive today, as a population, they have largely converted to Catholicism. (Some are Protestant.) While they remember their cultural beliefs and practices, they do not honor them as sacred any longer. Instead, those beliefs and practices are re-enacted at festivals to remember their past. (It's assumed, since Christianity currently rules their morality that there has been a fair amount of whitewashing regarding the homosexual elements of these practices at these re-enactments.)

I see no reason why rituals and tools that are affirming of homosexuality should have to lay fallow and unattended simply because Christianity has robbed our world of yet another beautiful tribal culture. There are countless white men and women joining the African Traditional Religions (ATRs) in droves, because Christianity isn't fulfilling their needs. In fact, the ATRs have practically been forced to accept white men and women to preserve their traditions, because people of African descent are leaving the traditional practices of their people to assimilate into mainstream Western Culture. Personally, I refuse to let the energetic current of something as beautiful and as affirming for Gay men as the Bullroarer Ceremony's symbolism to die out simply because it is not Christian-approved.

Fourth, and finally, the bullroarer has transcended its role as a sacred tool. It is for sale commercially on websites, in stores, and in public market places the world over. Today, it's purpose has extended beyond its sacred use into the realm of recreation. Given this fact, it makes no more sense to say that someone is culturally appropriating the bullroarer than it does to say that someone is culturally appropriating the car.

While you can certainly purchase a bullroarer for around $10, most witches prefer to make their own tools whenever possible. The choice of materials, the time and effort put into working out the details, and the time spent crafting the tool in question makes it unique to the individual witch. Some argue that this process of self-construction actually imbues the tool with added power.

Personally, though I am "crafty," I am not necessarily a handy witch. On occasion, I have found craft projects that interest me—knitting and blacksmithing immediately come to mind, but on the whole they just leave me frustrated and feeling bad about my lack of talent. I would rather have a well-made tool done by someone else that looks and feels good to me then fumble around like a rhesus lab monkey on crack and come up with an inferior product that constantly reminds me of my inadequacy. That only feels like adding insult to injury. Not only could I not muster up the basic mechanical skills to cut a straight line, but now I also have to suffer a deformed magical tool. No thank you!

If you happen to be handy and you want to construct your own bullroarer, the instructions for how to do so are below. Yes, I forced myself to try them. The results weren't awful. If you would rather not kick yourself while you're down and you can find a bullroarer for purchase that calls to you, go for it. Who am I to judge?

Instructions:

- Block of wood between 6 and 24 inches long and at least a quarter inch thick (can be thicker). Look for planks in the scrap box.
- Artificial sinew, real sinew, or paracord that is roughly 2-3 feet in length. It can be longer if you like, but avoid making the cord longer than you are tall—that way you don't run the risk of the bullroarer hitting the ground when you whirl it above your head.
- Saw (You can do this with a hand saw, but I highly recommend using a band saw if you have access to one.)
- Sandpaper (or belt sander)
- Drill

The bullroarer is really quite simple and easy to build. Generally, they are made of a hard wood with significant weight (not pine or cedar).

1. Make sure your wood is symmetrical. You want to draw basic lines to turn the rectangular wood into an oval. I recommend drawing a convex line in each of the 4 corners of your

rectangular piece of wood. This will give you the beginnings of your oval shape.
2. Remove the edges of the rectangle, which are outside the convex lines with the saw. BE CAREFUL OF YOUR FINGERS! Depending on how big the piece of wood you choose is, your hands may be close to the blade.
3. You will have a rough shape vaguely like the end product at this point, but it will need to be smoothed out and sanded down. Use a coarse grit sandpaper to start, and watch your corners carefully, maintaining symmetry.
4. Double check its symmetry by tracing it on a piece of paper and measuring the shape on the paper.
5. Once you have accounted for symmetry, the next step is to turn your flat oval into an airfoil. (Basically, that means you are going to round out the top and bottom flat surfaces of your oval. You want it to be fat in the center and thin on the edges, like a knife, an airplane wing, or the stereotypical image of a UFO.) If you use a belt sander, this will be easier, but it can be done with handheld sandpaper as well. Keep an even pressure, holding the object at a shallow angle against the sandpaper. Only work on one half at a time, maintaining symmetry as you do. Repeat the process on the other side.
6. Drill a hole in the middle of one end, about half an inch or so from the edge. This will be where you attach the cordage. Use a high-speed drill, applying low amounts of pressure to avoid splitting the wood.
7. Thread the cord, and practice with your tool to see if it makes the characteristic bullroarer sound. There are plenty of YouTube videos set up to teach you how to make the sound happen if your tool is constructed properly.

9 DEDICATION RITUAL

After you have developed your psychic talent and visualization skills, set a date for your ritual at least 14 days away. You will have a lot to do in this next fortnight, both mundanely and spiritually. You may even need more than 14 days to accomplish it all. If you do, take the extra time. You will need to spend time in regular meditation, contemplating the Archetypal Male and how he is reflected in you. Do your best to love yourself and see the beauty that already exists in you. See yourself as someone worthy of being emulated by others. Seeing yourself in this positive light is essential for the success of this ritual. While you're preparing yourself through meditation, it is advisable that you put in some practice with your bullroarer to gain a little proficiency with this tool. Make your dedication incense blend A.S.A.P., if you haven't already. Don't save this detail till the very last minute. You want to give it time for the ingredients to mingle properly.

Ideally, you would look for a secluded crossroads where you feel comfortable being naked. That means that you would have a reasonable expectation of privacy. For people who live out in the country, this may be easier than it is for people who live in an urban environment, but even the largest metropolis has access to camp grounds for rent if you look hard enough.

For some of us, doing this ritual out in nature simply will not be possible. Either health issues, location, or financial constraints will pose an insurmountable problem. Do what you can, and don't beat yourself up if you can't meet every criteria exactly. Get creative and use your imagination. You can create a crossroads in your living room very simply by placing 4 candles (in appropriate holders) in an X or equal-armed cross pattern within your room. Line the roads up with the directions. (Four-way roads tend to work better for the Male Mysteries, as three-way roads are viewed to be more feminine in nature.) You can construct your own sign post and use it as the phallus for the ritual instead of the herm that I suggest. You really are only limited by your creative imagination.

Please do me a favor, though, and do not risk getting put on the sex offender list by being caught naked out in public just to dedicate yourself to the Male Mystery Path. Nobody benefits from that—not you, not the Gods, nobody! Be smart, be conscious of your environment, and heed the laws of the land where you live.

Once you have the location established, you will need to construct your altar. The altar for the Male Mysteries is deceptively simple. However, as you will see, it is extremely powerful and versatile. At its most basic level, without any seasonal or ritual adornments, it is a **fire** with a **Herm** to the East and the **Black Rock of the Goddess** (or simply **The Black Rock**) to the West of it.

The first piece of the altar is a large phallic shaped stone to serve as your Herm. The shape of this stone can be as abstract or stylized as you want, like the Shiva Lingams that are often for sale in metaphysical stores, or it can be as literal as you desire. Provided you can find one, your Herm can even be more like the traditional style. (Traditional Herms are busts from the neck up with a square pillar as the base. The base frequently has phallic markings on it.) Whatever style Herm you choose, make sure it is substantial enough to draw your attention but still small enough that you can work with it easily. You'll need to be able to access the entire Herm while working this ritual, so do your knees a favor: make the Herm of an appropriate size so that you don't find yourself constantly standing and kneeling, like a Catholic at Mass.

The Black Rock is symbolic of Cybele's meteorite, which the Roman's brought back to their city to expel Hannibal from their home. Ideally, this stone would be made of iron-ore, as it is the Earth Mother's menstrual secretion, and harkens back to the very roots of the Male Mysteries. However, if you can get your hands on a sizable chunk of meteorite, that would also work. In a pinch, even a regular, old rock painted black will work.

In addition to your altar setup, you will want to have a witch's **broom** (better it be made from real broom straw), which should be kept somewhere easily accessible within your designated ritual space. In the North, have a small earthen bowl filled with **coins**—both domestic and foreign. Try to have coins from all corners of the globe if possible. The older, the better. (Banks will exchange your money for foreign currency.) North-West of your altar, position a small jar of good quality **honey**, ready to go. West of the altar, have a **chalice** of water. (Make sure to have additional water tucked away somewhere readily on hand should you have need of it.) Place a **green candle** (and **brass candlestick**) South of the altar unanointed, but ready to go.

Your **bullroarer** and appropriate incense take up the East.

A lovely incense, which has been aligned for the purposes of this ritual, consists of one pinch each of ground carnation flowers and of ground clover leaf added to ground copal. You want copal to be the dominant scent in this blend. It is only the essence of the other two plants, not necessarily their smell, which is called for here. With that in mind, mix these 3 ingredients according to your personal tastes. Then add just enough essential oil of Orange to slightly dampen the mixture. No more. Seal in a glass jar, and put away out of the light for at least 2 weeks.

Carnation is traditionally associated with Gay men for good reason. Just like Gay men are magical dynamos, so is this particular herb; it adds "oomph" to any incense blend. Clover is a masculine herb, sacred to the Triple Goddess, which brings youth, beauty, and health. It's balance of the Masculine and Feminine energies couldn't be passed over when constructing this blend. Copal is both loving and purifying, and it gives off a pleasant aroma as it burns. Finally, orange, which is often called "the fruit of joy," has so many wonderful uses that it would be impossible to list them all. However, for the purposes of this ritual, orange attracts abundance and happiness. Focus on those qualities as you add the oil to your mixture.

In the North-East, it would be appropriate to have your **fascinum charm necklace**, waiting for its use in your ritual. You may also choose to have as many illuminator candles as is necessary for you to be able to see effectively. (If you are doing this outside with a bonfire, you may not need any other light. However, if you modify the ritual to be done indoors, a few extra candles may be appreciated.) While a darker atmosphere is always very witchy, losing your place and stumbling around is not. So, either memorize the ritual or give yourself the extra illumination. You will also want the Witch's Liquor,[27] which can be placed anywhere that it will be easily accessible when needed. Make sure to have a clean towel on hand as well.

One final note before you begin. With the exception of the original action with the witch's broom, you will move widdershins during this ritual. Widdershins (counter-clockwise) energy attracts to you. Since you want to attract the attention of the Gods and the Spirits who oversee the Male Mysteries, and since you want to bring their wisdom

---

[27] The recipe follows the dedication ritual.

into your life, it is advisable that you move widdershins. Whenever you are called to move around your space, start in the North Quarter and move widdershins back to the North quarter before returning to the South Side of the fire. Conversely, deosil (or clockwise) energy uses the positive forces or the electric current to push away from or banish that which is already there. Hence starting this ritual by moving the broom deosil around your ritual space. Start in the East and move full-circle back to the East.

At midnight on a night of Mercury during the waxing moon, perform your rite. Spend that day in quiet contemplation, preparing for the ritual. Avoid any sexual stimulation for at least 24 hours before the ritual begins. Better that you abstain from any kind of sex for 3 solid days prior. Show up to your ritual naked.

As the clock tolls the midnight hour, light the fire. Do that first so that it will be ready for use during the ritual.

Take up your witch's broom and walk deosil around the designated ritual space, moving East to East. As you sweep the area, banish any forces that are not in alignment with your will this night:

> "Here, I conjure and command thee. By the might
> and power of my gods, Cybele and Dionysus, who
> are strong and just, I exorcise thee. Let only the
> good remain herein."

Take up the bowl of coins, and circumambulate widdershins, moving North to North around the ritual space, placing one coin at each of the pathways before you, saying:

> "By this sacred element, I conjure forth the riches
> of the Earth. The luck of my Gay ancestors now
> makes its way to me."

Replace the bowl of coins near the altar. Pick up the chalice of water and lightly asperge the space as you tread around saying:

> "Cleanse this sacred space, making it a fit and
> pleasing receptacle for the work I do here this
> night."

Set the chalice back down in its place. Circumambulate one whole cycle widdershins around the fire, saying:

> "May this light serve as a beacon to call the Old
> Gods and all who tend the Male Mysteries in good
> faith."

Pick up the bowl of incense, holding it aloft as you circumambulate widdershins from the North, saying:

> "May this sweet fragrance only attract good spirits
> to aid and guide me on my journey through the
> Male Mysteries."

Toss a handful of the incense into the fire. Return the bowl of incense to its spot. Suffumigate the fire as often as you like during the ritual.

You have now created a sacred space for the rite you will do here this night.

Put on drumming music and dance around the space, allowing yourself to trance out. (If your health makes it impossible for you to dance at this time, replace the drumming soundtrack with a real drum, and lose yourself in the rhythm you create with your own musical instrument.) The drum is the heartbeat of nature. Feel it. Be one with it.

Toss more incense into the fire, reaffirming that the smoke only invites helpful spirits and that it keep out harmful ones. Pick up the bullroarer, and swing it above your head widdershins as you focus on your call to the spirits. Mentally affirm for yourself to only invite good spirits to you, and see yourself protected by the God and Goddess. After you have a good "roar" going, say with confidence and conviction:

> "I call to the powerful and loving Gay spirits.
> Shaman, medicine men, healers all. I ask your aid,
> heed my call. Come to me this holy night, guide
> my way toward wisdom's light."

As the bullroarer hums through the air, see the spirits of powerful, loving Gay male ancestors come to join your rite. Then slowly let the bullroarer begin to wind down. After the call is over, place the bullroarer back in its spot near the fire. (If you can't swing the bullroarer, hold the paper, and speak the words, it is okay to break this part up in any way that makes sense to you.)

Hold the Witch's Liquor up to the sky, saying:

> "Great Mountain Mother, heal me of my madness.
> Teach me the joys of ecstasy and the sweet release
> of your wisdom."

Pour some of the liquor over the Black Rock and drink a little bit yourself (or, if you can't drink alcohol, pour some on the earth).

Take up your fascinum charm. Place the necklace around the Herm, and say:

> "Phallic Lord, grant your protection unto me.
> Protect me from all harm sent my way. Punish him
> who flings the curse. Turn evil back on its sender,
> and keep me safe through all of my days."

Pick up the jar of honey. Pour it over the Herm, and, as you bathe the Herm (and the charm) in honey, say:

> "May I be blessed with all the sweetness this life
> has to offer."

Pick up the bowl of coins and pour them out around the base of the Herm in a circular motion, moving widdershins until the bowl is empty. Say:

> "Money flow, money grow!" (Repeat as many
> times as it takes to empty the bowl.)

Now, turn your thoughts to the Archetypal Masculine. You have been meditating about your connection to this force over the past fortnight, so take a moment in quiet reflection now to conjure up the many similarities you share. See yourself as someone to be admired. Recognize your gifts—physical, emotional, mental, and spiritual. When you whole-heartedly believe in your worth as a man, begin to pleasure yourself.

Recognize that these are the traits that the Horned God of Witches, represented here by Dionysus, sees in you, and these are the traits about you that he loves. Recognize that, in this moment, you are his lover. Imagine how the two of you might interact with each other, and pleasure yourself to the fantasy.

Start slowly. Let the sexual energy build. When you can't hold back any longer, release your energy, visualizing all your wonderful attributes being contained within your semen.

Take a single drop of your semen, and place it in the chalice of water. (If you have to refill the water, do so.) Soma is the gift of the gods. This solitary drop, turns the water into an ambrosia-like substance. Drink it, and become more like your Horny lover. Your bliss was propelled by his divine spark, after all!

Take the remaining semen and rub it on your green candle. Go from the wick down to the center and from the bottom up to the center of the candle. As you anoint the candle with your essence, say:

> "As the light dispels the shadows, let this candle dispel the shadow of deceit and falsehood from my eyes. Let its light expel all stupidity and sloth from my mind, removing the obstacles to wisdom. Let it cast its illumination upon my heart so that I may understand love and grace. Blessed be!"

Place the green candle back in the brass candlestick. Light it, and sit in quiet contemplation regarding your experience. Let the candle burn down till it is just a nub. (If you can't stay in your location for that length of time, at least burn the candle for 15 minutes while you meditate in front of it.) Before the candle would go out on its own, extinguish it (do not blow it out!), and save the nub to light the next green candle, which should be anointed in the same manner. Whenever you work the Male Mysteries, light the green candle to guide your way.

In a heartfelt manner that feels appropriate to you, release the ancestors. Then release the gods. Thank them all for witnessing this rite of yours. If you already have a method that works for you, feel free to use it. If not, it is simply enough to say, "Thank you" or "Merry Meet and Merry Part Until We Merry Meet Again" while visualizing them leaving.

It's always a good idea to close down anything you open up. When you're ready to leave your sacred space, repeat the banishing ritual with the broom that started this ritual. Move deosil from East to East, repeating the petition. Then go enjoy a nice meal! After the ritual, wear the fascinum charm for protection.

WITCH'S LIQUOR

- 1 liter of grappa
- 2/3 cup granulated sugar
- Lemon rind
- 1/4 cup whole coffee beans

1. Slowly add the sugar to the grappa, stirring consistently until the sugar dissolves.
2. Add the lemon peel and the coffee beans, and stir again.
3. Bottle it in a sterilized container and use it for ritual purposes.

FIRE FESTIVALS

The peasants of Europe have kindled bonfires since time immemorial. How often these fires occurred and when throughout the year they were celebrated varies from region to region. The most common celebrations happened between the first of May and the Summer Solstice. While there are certainly customs surrounding the autumnal fires associated with both the harvest and the dead (especially in Celtic regions), there is very little information associated with the fire festivals of Midwinter (also called *the Winter Solstice*), which is odd considering the two main anthropological theories surrounding these rites.

The first of the theories surrounding the fire festivals is that they were a bit of sympathetic magic meant to encourage the sun to shine favorably upon the earth. As the terrestrial fires were kindled, the solar fires would spark to life. If this theory were true, it would only make sense that there would, in fact, have been fires around the Winter Solstice, since both solstices marked key turning-points associated with the sun throughout its yearly course. The Winter Solstice marks the darkest point of the year, when people would need the light and warmth from the sun the most. The Summer Solstice marks the point where the sun's power is at its height, and, naturally, people would have wanted to take advantage of that energy for the coming harvest. However, the literature and research backing this assumption up appears to be as scarce as the wintery landscape. While James Frazer dedicates quite a bit of his *Golden Bough* to discussing the spring and summer fires, he says comparatively little regarding their wintery counterparts.

The strongest argument in favor of this theory (often called *The Solar Theory of the Fire Festivals* or just *The Solar Theory*) is the dates of the festivals themselves. The two main fires being timed to coincide with the highest and the lowest points in the sun's celestial journey. While modern scholarship seems to lack sufficient documentation of specific customs and rituals surrounding the Midwinter Rites, there is plenty of archeological and anthropologic evidence that something did occur at this time. Consider Stonehenge and other monuments like it. The sympathetic components of these rites cannot be overlooked when considering them within the Solar Theory. In truth, the sympathetic magic explanation makes up the bulk of the argument. The construction of the need-fire through friction is often used as an argument in favor of this theory, because the sympathetic act of producing flame where there was no flame before would "show the sun" what people required of it. However, not every need-fire was constructed through the use of friction. As its name suggests, need-fires were kindled whenever the people had *need* of them, mostly in times of distress. It is natural to assume that a fire kindled *in need* would favor the most expedient method of combustion that the populace had available to them at the time. The final point in this argument is that the seasonal fires were intended to act as weather charms to bring favorable weather and abundant crops. For example, the belief that lighting a bonfire in the month of June will cause the rain to disappear. The Swiss believed that the fires would clear away clouds and bring back the sunshine.

The second theory regarding the fire festivals is that they were rites of purification. This theory is the more favored of the two. The strongest argument for this theory is that the people who actually practice the fire festivals seem to allege this theory in explanation of their activities. They drive their herds and flocks through the smoke to purify them of disease; they use the smoke and ashes to purify the land, and they jump the flames themselves (both for good luck and purification). Another argument in favor of this theory is that it is simpler. The conception of fire as a destructive force is so simple that even a child can understand it. Animals run in fear of fire. Unrestrained fire can burn away our homes and communities in a matter of hours. It is also natural to endeavor to repurpose the destructive aspects of fire for the use of man. However, the sympathetic link between terrestrial fire and the sun is far less obvious, requiring some rather complex thought. While this theory also accounts for the fire's ability to control the weather, it does so in a protective (instead of a generative) capacity. The bonfires were believed to have the power to protect the fields from hale and the homestead from lightning.

Modern witches like to refer to themselves as *Pagans*. This most likely stems from the belief that it will avoid antagonizing other non-witches. In truth, there's nothing wrong with it. It's become a useful label to unite the disparate communities who currently rally under that modern Pagan umbrella. The only argument against it is historical. Pagans maligned and murdered witches just as much as the Christians did. The purification theory of the fire festivals is a prime example. A great many of the customs associated with purification at these rites were designed to protect against or undo the effects of a witch's curse: passing the herds through the smoke, hurling flaming disks into the air to knock the invisible witches off of their brooms, or even spreading the protective ash across the fields to prevent blight—these were all precautions against witchcraft. However, tradition alone has never been a good-enough reason to do or not do anything. That's especially the case with the adoption or avoidance of a label. If it serves a useful purpose for witches alive today to call themselves *Pagan* (in order to keep the peace or otherwise), I, personally, don't see a problem with it, provided we remember our history.

The rites listed below take that exact philosophy. I don't know whether the original fire festivals were solar-inspired or whether they were designed to purify the people, the animals, and the land. I don't care. Both elements seem useful to modern Gay male witches, and that's all I'm currently concerned with. That is why you will find both elements interwoven within the seasonal rites below.

As you study this material, you will find a simple Need-Fire Rite. Whether you kindle your fire the traditional way or you use a lighter is irrelevant to me or to the work itself. As I said, the fact that the need-fires were kindled in times of distress probably meant that the people kindling them operated through expediency. If our ancestors had lighters or matches, I am willing to bet they would have used them from time to time.

You will also find four seasonal rites. Though they are meant to be done at the solstices and equinoxes, you can do them any time between the Cross-Quarter and the Quarter Days, as they are seasonal rites meant to align your energy with the energy of the seasons where you live.

CRAFTING PETITIONS

For modern witches, petitions are generally burned as a part of the Fire Festival theme. Typically, they are written on paper with pencil and tossed in the fire. However, I have provided an interesting method below, which you are free to adopt as your own during your fire festivals (or other magical workings), as you feel compelled.

The petitions that are written for these rites should be the result of real internal soul-searching. It's not enough to merely look inside yourself. As a witch, we recognize the natural ebb and flow. There is an appropriate time for certain types of energies, and, during that time, addressing those energies becomes easier than it might be at other times. Nowhere is this truer than when we turn inward and confront ourselves. Be a witch. Don't fight the natural cycles. Instead, recognize what energies are present in each season and learn to turn them to your advantage for your own personal growth and development. By aligning yourself with the energies of the seasons, you will not only gain peace and calm within yourself, you will also grow in power and wisdom.

Some seasonal rites start in Spring, because it is when the first signs of life emerge from their wintery slumber. Other cycles favor winter as the starting point, because all life starts in darkness. The seed beneath the ground is nurtured by the earth until it sprouts forth. The baby in the mother's womb is another common example. Even ideas start as nebulous concepts in the blackness of the subconscious mind, only emerging into the consciousness after thy have gained a sufficient amount of energetic force to be able to thrive in the light.

For the Male Mysteries (in general), I favor starting in winter, because the sun (light/fire) is at its lowest point, and it is easiest to see the wheel turn from that point. The sun is faint in winter. It waxes stronger in spring, even stronger throughout the summer, and it begins to wan again in autumn, continuing its decline back down to its lowest point through the depth of winter. However, that is not an essential starting point. As I said, there are two prominent philosophies on this point, so if the spring philosophy makes more sense to you, you can certainly start there.

Regardless of where you choose to start your particular spin of the Wheel, the energies associated with the season are thus:

> **Winter**—this is the best time to clear away the old and make room for the new. If it no longer serves you, get rid of it.
> **Spring**—this is the time for new beginnings. Plant the seeds of things you want to manifest in your life.
> **Summer**—this is the perfect time to nurture those spring seeds, which have begun to flower in your life. It's also an excellent time for weeding out the excess "weeds," which are crowding out or stifling the growth of the desirable things you actually want to encourage in the garden that is your life.
> **Autumn**—this is when you take stock of the situation, account for your successes, and catalogue the places where you failed to achieve the desired results. It's also a good time to do any "course corrections," and get back on track with your goals.

Ultimately, the process for writing the petitions for these rites is basically the same. Give yourself a solid week or two for the process when you're just starting out. You may need that long to wrap your head around the concept of crafting effective petitions. Allow yourself the time and space to learn. If something isn't glaringly obvious, it will become so in due time. That's why you're giving yourself at least a week or two.

Spend some time looking over your life before each rite. Compare your present situation against the basic themes listed above. For example, don't try to kill off a bad habit in spring. (That's a better petition for winter.) Instead, open the way for a good habit to take its place.

Use clear, concise, simple, modern language to craft the intention. Like your affirmations, write the petition in positive language in the present tense. "I am a successful blacksmith" instead of "I will be a successful blacksmith." This is not the place for flowery or poetic language. Be plain. Keep it simple.

NEED-FIRE RITE

In addition to the Pagan festivals of Europe, there is another important influence upon these rites, which must be explored. Rather than being folkloric, this second influence is mythic. While I have already talked about the symbolism of the light (fire) within the Male Mysteries, it is the mythic connection, more than anything else, which reveals the centrality of the fire festivals to a Gay male witch's celebrations of the seasons.

There are two sacred Hindu texts, which are generally viewed to be the origin of petitioning the fire within the Male Mysteries. *The Mahabharata* says that Kartikeya was formed of Shiva's energy "entering into" Agni. Kartikeya is, therefore, son to both gods. The epic goes on to describe Kartikeya as the leader of an all-male army. He is described as having the ability to reproduce on his own without the intercession of any female. *The Shiva Purana*, a later text, is the source of the more detailed description of this birth. Whereas the first text euphemizes the encounter, the second text states it outright. Agni provides oral sex to Shiva, and Kartikeya is born when Agni swallows Shiva's semen.

Agni is not just the god of fire in Hindu mythology. He actually is fire! Whenever there is fire, Agni is present. It is for this reason that a common method of petitioning the gods within the Male Mysteries involves ejaculating into the fire. (It sympathetically reproduces the action of the mythic act of homosexual creation.) Since it might be difficult to get close enough to actually ejaculate directly into a roaring fire, we'll be using a variation of this practice within these rites.

Rather than risk life and limb, so to speak, it is highly advisable that you construct a *petition poppet*. A few days (or as far out as two weeks) prior to the ritual, concentrate on your particular goal, pleasuring yourself in the privacy of your own home. After you have achieved release, collect the "blood of the lion"[28] on virgin cloth. The cloth is thereafter known as *the pearl towelette*. Once the pearl towelette has dried

---

[28] A euphemistic way that many witches talk about semen.

thoroughly, construct the poppet by cutting its pattern out of the pearl towelette, making sure to include the blood of the lion on at least one side of what will become the poppet.

When the petition is constructed as a poppet, you will want to stuff herbs appropriate to the particular season or ritual, a written version of your petition (crafted in accordance with the directions above), and any remaining fabric from the pearl towelette. It's always advisable to construct the poppet so the blood of the lion is on the inside of the doll, but each witch may do as he please.

The basic structure of these fire festivals is always the same. During the Seasonal Rites, you would simply plug the seasonal actions into the generic Need-Fire Rite given below. The Seasonal Rites below are written to be complete, incorporating the Need-Fire Rite within them. This is done to show you how you can modify things yourself to accomplish a complete and effective ritual using just the Need-Fire Rite. The Need-Fire Rite can be used at any time that you have **need of it**. It is a wonderful ritual structure for any spellwork, but healing, luck, and protection rituals are most traditional.

The altar, which at its most basic is the Need-Fire, the Black Stone to the West of the Fire, and the Herm to the East, is set in the middle of the ritual space so that the witch may dance around it easily without obstruction. The altar may be embellished according to the needs of the ritual or spell. Any incense may be tossed directly into the Need-Fire to suffumigate the ritual space. Though this rite is designed to be done outside, it is often difficult for modern witches to take their workings out into nature. When the obstacles prove too great for the witch to overcome, it is advisable to perform the rite inside, making whatever modifications are necessary for a smooth transition.

(1) Begin the ritual by preparing yourself and the ritual space according to the needs of the rite.

(2) Engage in a light dance. Move deosil to protect or project outward. Move widdershins to attract to yourself. With few exceptions, most of the rituals in this book call for your dances to be accompanied exclusively with the drum. As these are solitary rites, it would be advisable for the practicing witch to purchase some drumming music that calls to his spirit, and use that during ritual. If a witch can't dance because of health reasons or space limitations, it is always permissible to replace dancing with drumming in real time (or even meditation). In the case of covens or groups of Gay and Bisexual male witches

working these rites together, it might be a good idea to designate a drummer or two to keep a beat for the ritual dancers.

Next appeal to the gods. (3) Start with the Goddess. This honors the historical fact that the Male Mysteries developed out of the Female Mysteries and that it is from manipulation of the menstrual secretions of the Earth Mother, herself (represented by the Black Rock), that we, as Gay male witches, originally claimed our own right to power. After whatever invocations or ritualized honoring you choose, some rituals may call for you to pour the Witch's Liquor over the Black Rock in reverence. That recipe can be found right after the dedication ritual. I highly recommend having a ready supply constantly on hand. Some rituals may even ask you to anoint the kindling with the remaining liquor before lighting the fire.

(4) Make any appeals to the God (whether invocation, words of respect, or visualizations), which are appropriate for your specific rite. Kindle the fire to bring his presence fully into your ritual space.

After you have invoked the energies of the gods, (5) perform the actual working. In the case of spellwork, you would put the actions of the spell here. Simply follow the directions of the spell itself before finishing out the remainder of the Need-Fire Rite.

(6) End the Need-Fire Rite with any appropriate acts of revelry. Remember the Male Mysteries and witchcraft are ecstatic in nature. Let yourself go. Dance, sing, drum, make merry around the fire as long as you feel called to do so. Make sure to close everything down in the opposite order in which you opened it. Basically, that means if you invoke something, release it. If you open something, close it. (7) Include a feast with good food, fine wine, and social pleasures whenever possible.

The Need-Fire right is necessarily barebones. I did this on purpose to encourage you to use your own creativity. As Gay men, one of our universal gifts is our creativity. I do not want to stifle that beauty in you by giving you so many rules that you feel uncomfortable embellishing these rites and rituals. Enjoy expressing your uniqueness. Enjoy exercising your creativity. Make your rituals and spells beautiful. Make them powerful, but most of all make them your own. Treat them as gifts you give the gods, whom you worship.

While these rites are written to be done outside, like the Dedication, they can be modified to be done indoors with some careful thought and planning. Instead of logs, you might use an appropriately colored candle situated within a cauldron. While you may not be able to burn the petition poppet up with such a small flame, you can arrange to eliminate it in other ways appropriate to your rite, either saving the burning for after the ritual or whatever else calls to your circumstances.

You will notice that the Winter Rite is a bit different when it comes to the hymns to the gods than the other 3 rites. The other 3 rites have hymns chosen directly from the 1792 Thomas Taylor translation of *The Orphic Hymns*, whereas the hymns to the gods in the Winter Rite are creative modifications of gems from that same book mixed with my own creativity. I have done this on purpose to show you how you can handle your own rites. I highly recommend that you get yourself a copy of *The Orphic Hymns*, regardless of translation. They are worth their weight in gold when it comes to invocations and petitioning the gods.

If you find something so beautiful that it calls to your soul, use it. There's probably a reason. Just replace the hymn I put there as a placeholder with the one you like more. If you find something that is sort of "on-point" but doesn't completely hit the mark for your rite, modify it appropriately for your situation. And, if you have the talent or the desire to do so, write your own. Since there are so many beautiful hymns and invocations out there already, I didn't feel the need to write my own for these rites.

These rites are meant to enhance your spirituality and align you with the Male Mysteries. If you do them exactly as written, that will happen. Once you get comfortable with their energies, you may want to expand beyond their limited borders. That's okay too. Hopefully, you will get a lot of use out of these rites for years to come, but if you have to modify things to suit your particular needs or the needs of your coven, do so.

You will notice that I do not use the names for the Goddess and the God. This, too, is on purpose. I want to help you connect with the Great Goddess and the Great God in any guise that appeals to you. Feel free to replace the titles used with specific names that call to you if you want to do that. Also feel free to work with the hymns as they are written. They will work either way.

Finally, I use the title *Adonis* to refer to the God in these rites. That is not meant to refer to the beautiful Greek youth, though it certainly could if you feel called to work with him. He was a vegetation god, initially. That god's actual name is Tammuz. Adonis, like Adonai, is a title, simply another word for *Lord*. Since Adonis is so appealing to Gay men, and since many Gay men struggle with Christianity, I have chosen to replace *Adonai*, a common title for God, with *Adonis*, instead. Wherever the God is actually named within the hymns, I have chosen to substitute the title *Adonis* instead of names or other possible titles.

WINTER RITE

Many of the gods of the Male Mysteries were once worshipped as tree spirits. Dionysus, Tammuz (who we just discovered went by the title Adonis), and Attis—all were heavily associated with trees, specifically the pine tree. Their connection to this powerful symbol of everlasting life has been represented here by the use of the evergreen bough.

Various cultures ascribed various powers to trees and the tree spirits who inhabited them. Some thought they brought rain and sunshine. Others thought that the spirits within the trees could make crops grow. Regardless of what powers were actually attributed to the trees, themselves, the simple fact remains that trees were viewed to be potent powers. Considering that they spend their entire existence absorbing, transmuting, and dispersing the Earth Mother's magnetism, that makes sense. Like the blacksmith, trees take the Earth Mother's energies and transmute them into a phallic structure. (Trees as giant poles sticking out of the ground certainly qualify as phallic!)

For this rite, you will need all the usual altar supplies (the Black Rock, the Herm, the bonfire), but you will also need an **anointing oil** of both clove and orange. Add 1-3 drops of clove oil and 9 drops of orange to 1 ounce of carrier oil.[29] Build your bonfire out of 9 different woods. A **black candle** for the ritual torch. **Wreath** made from evergreen bough. Any items necessary to decorate your wreath. The **Potion of Rebirth**.[30] A **petition poppet** stuffed with **herbal mixture** of storax, bay leaves, ground star anise, clove, coriander, and 6 pomegranate seeds. Take any remaining herbal mixture and use it as incense in the bonfire.

A few days prior to the ritual, you will want to cut yourself a bough of evergreen, which you can fashion into a wreath. Make sure to give the wreath a few days to dry. You want to give the pine time to dry so that your fire doesn't spark unnecessarily, but you don't want your

---

[29] Play with these ratios till you produce a smell that is pleasing to you. If you have any allergies, make any necessary substitutions.
[30] Recipe follows this rite.

wreath sitting so long that it begins to shed its needles.

The circle is the most efficient shape for moving energy, and since our goal is to rekindle the light as quickly as possible, the unbroken circle is perfect for this rite. Decorate your wreath as the spirit of the season calls to you. Some good options might be green, red, and white ribbons, pinecones, holly leaves and berries.

(1) Begin the ritual by anointing yourself with the oil on your forehead. A good symbol to trace on yourself might be the Earth Banishing Pentagram, which is easily accessible online. Take the black candle and walk deosil around the ritual space, saying any words of banishment that call to you. You may use the words from the dedication rite if they call to you or you may find others more suitable to your work here this night.

(2) Dance lightly to get your energy up before (3) you recite the hymn to the Goddess:

> "Illustrious Goddess—sonorous, divine! Come
> blessed queen and to my rites incline: O venerable
> Goddess, source of eternal life, free me from this
> madness, relieve the frenzied strife! Born of the
> earth, beneath her crust you dwell, leash the dogs
> of war, and lock the gates of hell! Tend my
> wounded, weary soul, as you tend the Vine,
> embrace me with your gentle touch, and let my
> glory shine."[31]

Spend a few moments contemplating the healing energies of the Great Mother. How can she heal your wounds and put you back on course?

(4) Place the wreath of evergreen on the pyre as you recite the hymn to the God:

> "Bull-horn'd and lovely, undying God of earth,
> teach me the secrets of your great rebirth.
> Resplendent child of the corn, vintner to the vine,
> gardener to the blooming bud, and lord within the

---

[31] Modified from Hymns to Rhea and Persephone from *The Orphic Hymns*, translated by Thomas Taylor.

pine. At recurring points within each year, doomed to set and rise, the promise of a life renewed when the sun lights up the skies."[32]

Lift up a glass of the Potion of Rebirth, toss some of it on the pyre, and light the fire. Drink the rest of the Potion of Rebirth, partaking of the God's essence.

(5) Toss the poppet on the fire, and focus on your petition. Let go of everything that is no longer useful in your life. See it burn up with the poppet, clearing the way for a fresh cycle. Reflect on your past year. What has brought you to this point of death? What mistakes did you make over the last year? What lessons did you learn from them? How will you be reborn?

(6) End the night with revelry. Dance, sing, feast, and make merry! Make sure to leap the fire at least 3 times, but don't feel you have to stop there. Jump high!

---

[32] Modified from Hymns to Bacchus and Adonis from *The Orphic Hymns*, translated by Thomas Taylor.

POTION OF REBIRTH

- 1 bottle of red wine
- 24 oz pomegranate juice
- 1/3 cup of sugar
- 2/3 cup of water
- 2 inches of ginger root (sliced)
- 3 cinnamon sticks
- 6 allspice berries
- 2 star anise pods
- 1 orange sliced up

1. Create simple syrup out of water, sugar, and ginger. Let steep for 15 minutes before removing the ginger root.
2. Add to a pot with the other ingredients, and cook on low until ingredients have mingled their flavors (roughly 45 minutes).
3. Strain it before serving.

*If you want to add alcohol back in, you can always add more wine later and serve cold. If you don't care about the alcohol content, you can serve this delicious elixir while it's hot.

SPRING RITE

The ancient galli priests of Cybele and Attis castrated themselves with terra cotta shards during the Vernal Equinox. I don't know many Gay men who would be willing to go that far today. In truth, I don't know any men who would do it! So, today, we use a symbolic sacrifice of virility to strengthen the God's return and to stand in for the gorier practices of our ancestors.

For this rite, you will need **Almond Oil** for anointing. A **green candle** (not the candle you consecrated at your dedication, another one) to serve as a ritual torch. You will want to build your Need-Fire out of **Oak**, **Walnut**, and **Beech**, using **Broom** as kindling to start the fire. **Violet flowers** and any other **springtime herbs**, which are readily available in your location at the time. Use these herbs to stuff the **petition poppet**, and bring a bowl filled with the same herbs to your ritual. (Generally hyacinth, flax seed, and violets are used. Violet, however, is the only essential ingredient.) You will need a **working knife (flint)**. Have a **pomegranate** and a **diabetic lancet kit** on hand. (Do not share lancets and be careful of blood borne diseases. Take all proper medical precautions. If you aren't familiar with proper medical procedures for handling blood, do your research before engaging in this rite with anyone else.) You will also want **The Witch's Liquor** for this rite.

(1) Begin the rite by anointing yourself with oil drawing an Earth Banishing Pentagram on your forehead. Take the green candle and walk deosil around the ritual space, saying any words of banishment that call to you. You may use the words from the dedication ritual if they call to you or find others more suitable to your work here this night. The idea is that you are banishing death (Winter) from the land so that new life may bloom.

(2) Dance lightly deosil round the space to get your energy up before (3) appealing to the Goddess:[33]

---

[33] To Nature (X) from *The Orphic Hymns*, Translated by Thomas Taylor, p. 29.

"Nature, all parent, ancient, and divine,
O Much-mechanic mother, art is thine;
Heav'nly, abundant, venerable queen,
In ev'ry part of thy dominions seen.
Untam'd, all-taming, ever splendid light,
All ruling, honor'd, and supremely bright.
Immortal, first-born, ever still the same,
Nocturnal, starry, shining, glorious dame.
Thy feet's still traces in a circling course,
By thee are turn'd, with unremitting force.
Pure ornament of all the pow'rs divine,
Finite and infinite alike you shine;
To all things common and in all things known,
Yet incommunicable and alone.
Without a father of thy wond'rous frame,
Thyself the father whence thy essence came.
All-flourishing, connecting, mingling soul,
Leader and ruler of this mighty whole.
Life-bearer, all-sustaining, various nam'd,
And for commanding grace and beauty fam'd.
Justice, supreme in might, whose general sway
The waters of the restless deep obey.
Ætherial, earthly, for the pious glad,
Sweet to the good, but bitter to the bad.
All-wife, all bounteous, provident, divine,
A rich increase of nutriment is thine;
Father of all, great nurse, and mother kind,
Abundant, blessed, all-spermatic mind:
Mature, impetuous, from whose fertile seeds
And plastic hand, this changing scene proceeds.
All-parent pow'r, to mortal eyes unseen,
Eternal, moving, all-sagacious queen.
By thee the world, whose parts in rapid flow,
Like swift descending streams, no respite know,

> On an eternal hinge, with steady course
> Is whirl'd, with matchless, unremitting force.
> Thron'd on a circling car, thy mighty hand
> Holds and directs, the reins of wide command.
> Various thy essence, honor'd, and the best,
> Of judgement too, the general end and test.
> Intrepid, fatal, all-subduing dame,
> Life-everlasting, Parca, breathing flame.
> Immortal, Providence, the world is thine,
> And thou art all things, architect divine.
> O blessed Goddess, hear thy suppliant's pray'r,
> And make my future life, thy constant care;
> Give plenteous seasons, and sufficient wealth,
> And crown my days with lasting, peace and health."

Pour some of the Witch's Liquor over the Black Rock. Then toss the remainder over the kindling.

(4) Wedge the flint into the flesh of the pomegranate, being careful not to cut yourself. Separate the segments of the fruit, exposing the flesh and seeds, say:

> "Roused by rabid rage, his mind astray, with sharp
> flint downwards, the galli dashed his virility!"

Pour the pomegranate juices, flesh, and seeds over both the Black Rock and the Herm as an offering to the gods. As you pour the juices over the herm in this symbolic gesture (which stands in place of the more savage historic ritual), say:

> "Adonis, I offer this small sacrifice to thee in
> hopes that you will amplify my offering, granting
> me joy, ecstasy, and an excess of your own Godly
> virility in its place."

Then place the remainder of the pomegranate onto the ritual pyre so that it may sweeten the fire once it is kindled.

(5) Take a sterilized lancet, and ritually prick your finger. Anoint the

petition poppet with your blood. Then, (6) appeal to the God, [34]saying:

> "Much nam'd, and best of daemons, hear my
>   pray'r,
> The desert loving, deck'd with tender hair;
> Joy to diffuse, by all desired, is thine,
> Much form'd, Eubulus, aliment divine.
> Female and male, all-charming to the sight,
> Adonis, ever flourishing and bright;
> At stated periods doom'd to set and rise
> With splendid lamp, the glory of the skies?
> Two horn'd and lovely, reverenc'd with tears,
> Of splendid form, adorn'd with copious hairs.
> Rejoicing in the chase, all-graceful pow'r,
> Sweet plant of Venus, Love's delightful flow'r:
> Descended from the secret bed divine
> Of Pluto's queen, the fair-hair'd Proserpine.
> 'Tis thine to sink in Tartarus profound,
> And shine again thro' heav'ns illustrious round;
> Come, timely pow'r, with providential care,
> And to thy mystics earth's productions bear."

Place the poppet on the pyre, sprinkle any of the remaining seasonal herbs over the poppet, and light the fire with the green candle.

(7) End the night with revelry. Dance, sing, feast, and make merry! The final thing you should do that night before turning in is brew yourself a strong herbal infusion[35] made from chamomile, spearmint, and passionflower to help with a shamanic journey. Make sure you are not allergic to any of the ingredients of this edible potion. Check with a qualified medical professional if you are unsure, and make any substitutions that are appropriate for your situation. Mix it with honey, a slice of lemon, and a dash of nutmeg. Drink it, thinking about the Dying God and his return from the Underworld. It might be good to read some of the myths of Dionysus, Attis, or Adonis as you enjoy

---

[34] To Adonis (LVI) from *The Orphic Hymns*, Translated by Thomas Taylor, p. 115.
[35] Thank you Thorn Nightwind for this wonderful herbal blend!

your potion. Let these themes permeate your subconscious, and, then, when you are done, go immediately to sleep. When you wake up, write down any revelations, insights, or wisdom you gained from your nightly journey.

Save any ashes from the Spring Rite fire for use in your Summer Rite.

SUMMER RITE

The season most connected to the fire festival throughout Europe was Midsummer. There is a plethora of lore and customs associated with these celebrations. A central theme of the Midsummer fires was protection. People threw bones and filth of all sorts into the fire to make a foul smoke, presumably to drive away malevolent forces. The summer rites were also filled with customs designed to bring fertility, protection, and good health. It was believed that whoever jumped the fire 3 times during these rites would not suffer from fever during the course of that year. Leaping the fires during this time of year also had implications for the success of the coming harvest, and, in some cases, it served to foretell who would marry within the year. (Because of its protective associations, this is a wonderful time of year to recharge your fascinum charm if it begins to lose its potency.)

Things needed for this rite include a **gold candle** to serve as the ritual torch. A **petition poppet**. The **ashes** you saved from your Spring Rite will be brought out and used now. You will want to build you Need-Fire out of **9 different woods** and use **straw** as kindling to start it. Bring a bowl filled with **9 different herbs** to serve as your ritual **incense**. You will also need another bowl of **foul smelling herbs** (like sulfur). **The Witch's Liquor**! If you are going to recharge your **fascinum charm**, bring that too, along with a jar of the best quality **honey** you can afford.

Good options for the incense during this ritual are sage, mint, basil, tarragon, parsley, rosemary, thyme, hyssop, honeysuckle, sunflower, lavender, fern, mistletoe, St. John's Wort, meadowsweet, feverfew, iris. Some additional trees that can be used for constructing the fire are oak, rowan, birch, ash, alder, willow, hawthorne, holly, and hazel. Avoid elder!

Construct your petition poppet a few days in advance of the ritual according to our custom. Stuff the doll with **mugwort, vervain, and larkspur**. **Straw** may also serve as filler, in addition to the remainder of the pearl towelette.

(1) Begin the rite by smearing yourself with ashes then carry the golden torch and the petition poppet around the ritual space. Say any words of banishment that call to you. If nothing else, use the words of banishment from your dedication.

(2) Place the poppet on the pyre and light the Need-Fire with the gold candle. Toss bonemeal, sulfur, and other foul-smelling herbs into the fire to banish the forces of chaos and destruction, saying:

> "May all my ill-luck depart and be burnt up with thee!"

During this time, it would be appropriate to focus on the things you need to weed out of your personality or your life so that you may encourage the desirable energies to flourish within your life. If your petition cultivates something within yourself, see the burning of the poppet opening the way for success, removing the obstacles that have thus far held you back. If you wrote your petition to eliminate some undesirable quality or situation, simply see it burning away in the fire.

(3) Dance deosil around the fire. (4) Appeal to the Great Mother,[36] asking that she bless your rite, saying:

> "MOTHER of Gods, great nurse of all, draw near,
> Divinely honour'd, and regard my pray'r.
> Thron'd on a car, by lions drawn along,
> By bull-destroying lions, swift and strong.
> Thou sway'st the sceptre of the pole divine,
> And the world's middle seat, much fam'd, is thine.
> Hence earth is thine, and needy mortals share
> Their constant food, from thy protecting care.
> From thee at first both Gods and men arose;
> From thee the see and ev'ry river flows.
> Vesta and source of wealth thy name we find
> To mortal men rejoicing to be kind;
> For ev'ry good to give thy soul delights.
> Come, mighty pow'r, propitious to our rites,

---

[36] To The Mother of the Gods (XXVII) from *The Orphic Hymns*, translated by Thomas Taylor, p. 63.

> All-taming, blessed, Phrygian Saviour, come,
> Saturn's great queen, rejoicing in the drum.
> Celestial, ancient, life-supporting maid,
> Inspiring fury; give they suppliant aid;
> With joyful aspect on our incense shine,
> And pleas'd, accept the sacrifice divine."

Pour the Witch's liquor over the black rock (but, for fire safety reasons, don't add any to the Need-Fire this time, better that you drink it or pour it out on the earth as an offering to the Nature Spirits).

(4) Appeal to the God,[37] saying:

> "Terrestrial Adonis, hear my pray'r,
> Rise vigilant with Nymphs of lovely hair:
> Great Amphietus Adonis, annual God,
> Who laid asleep in Proserpine's abode,
> Her sacred seat, didst lull to drowsy rest
> The rites triennial and the sacred feast;
> Which rous'd again by thee mystic anthems sing;
> When briskly dancing with rejoicing pow'rs,
> Thou mov'st in concert with the circling hours.
> Come blessed, fruitful, horned, and divine,
> And on this sacred Telete propitious shine;
> Accept the pious incense and the pray'r,
> And make prolific holy fruits thy care."

(5) Toss the bowl of censing herbs onto the Need-Fire and, if needed, recharge the fascinum charm.

If you are going to recharge the fascinum charm, remove it, and, at this point in the ritual place the necklace around the Herm, saying:

> "Phallic Lord, grant your protection unto me.
> Protect me from all harm sent my way. Punish him
> who flings the curse. Turn evil back on its sender,

---

[37] To Amphietus Bacchus (LIII) from *The Orphic Hymns*, translated by Thomas Taylor, p. 111.

and keep me safe through all my days."

Reproduce the actions of your dedication, which originally empowered the charm. Pick up the jar of honey. Pour it over the Herm, and, as you bathe the Herm and charm in honey, say:

**"May I be blessed with all the sweetness this life
has to offer."**

(6) End the night with revelry. Dance, sing, feast, and make merry! Make sure to leap the fire at least 3 times.

AUTUMNAL RITE

My favorite name for this rite is *The Winnowing*. Not only does it sound dark and wonderfully witchy, but it gets to the very heart of the Harvest Rites for Gay men. It deals with a quintessential piece of the Male Mysteries: the mysteries of the corn and the importance of the wolf transformation.

In Eastern Europe, this wolf transformation eventually took on a werewolf-like quality. In fact, it is the mysteries of the corn from the Eastern European countries, which originally inspired our modern interpretation of the werewolf. In Western Europe, the werewolf transformation was never explicitly connected to the spirit of the corn, but the similarities between Eastern and Western practices in this regard provides a strong case for the origins of the spirit itself actually being the same.

In the Northern and Southern parts of Europe, the wolf spirit was more easily seen in the fighting classes. The warriors who worshipped Mars in Rome, embraced the mantle of the wolf, as the creature was sacred to the God of War. In the North, Odin had his berserkers, which also included Wolf Warriors.

Whether in agriculture (as we experience it here, in this rite) or in war, the wolf and the men who explore the Male Mysteries are intimately tied together. Finally, the Corn Wolf (as this spirit is often called) in the harvest mythologies of various European lands is also analogous to the ancient shamanic priesthood of the Goddess. In fact, the Luperci of ancient Rome were priests of the Old Religion who took their name from this type of symbolism.

In America, we tend to think of maize as corn. However, the word corn can be applied to the dominant grain throughout the region. In America, that grain was maize, which is why we think of maize as corn. In Europe, however, the dominant crop was either wheat, rye, barley, or rice. The Corn Wolf, then, is the spirit within a community's dominant crop.

Throughout Europe, the grain is guarded by a spirit in the guise of a wolf. He is the protector of the Earth Mother's bounty, and he generally has all the outward appearance of a regular, living wolf. This fact can be deduced by the many divinatory practices, which have sprung up around Europe regarding wolf sightings during this time of year. If a wolf is seen in or near the fields, he is an omen for either good or ill.

According to one legend, his fertilizing power resides in his tail. If he carries his tail high, it is a dreaded sign, meaning the harvest will be weak and feeble. However, if he drags his tail low on the ground, the immediate future holds many blessings.

The spirit of the harvest is not always a wolf. Alternately, it is a cock (rooster), hare, cat, goat, bull, or various other animals. It can even be a man. In fact, in many cases when folklore talks about the Corn Wolf, the reference is meant to describe the villager who cut or threshed the last stalk of grain. Due to the associations of the ancient wolf cult with homosexual priesthoods, I have chosen to honor the wolf spirit variety here. It reflects the ancient practice of priests shapeshifting for the protection of the community.

The witch plays the part of the Corn Wolf within this ritual. For this rite, you will need an **anointing oil** made of 2 drops coriander, 1 drop ginger, and 2 drops bergamot essential oils in 1 ounce of linseed carrier oil. Play with the ratios till you have a spicy, warm fragrance that calls to you. Be sparing with the ginger, though, as it can irritate the skin. Build your **Need-Fire** out of fruit trees (apple, walnut, grapevine, etc.) if at all possible. Ground up **myrrh resin** for your incense during this ritual. A **petition poppet** (an effigy of the Corn King) dressed up to look like a corpse. Herbs for this ritual are **red damask roses**, **wheat stalks**, **flax**, any other **grains**, **corn flower** (also called bachelor's buttons; its scientific name is centaurea cyanus), dried **corn husks**, and **turmeric**. Secure a jar of the best quality **honey** you can afford. You will also need a **skeleton key** on a small amount of **rope or cord**, a **chalice of water**, and, finally, you will want 3 liquors: **The Witch's Liquor**, **Beer**, and **Brandy**.

Construct the petition poppet (the Corn King) for this rite according to our custom. Stuff him full with the red damask roses, wheat, flax, the blue corn flowers, and any other grains you have on hand. Don't forget to put the written petition inside the poppet with what remains of the pearl towelette after you cut out the pattern. Dress the Corn King up like a corpse, and tie the skeleton key around his neck, giving him the power to symbolically unlock the mysteries of the corn. Pray over the body of the Corn King as you shower him with more of the blue corn flowers and the red damask roses. (Any remaining herbs can be saved to sweeten the Need-Fire.) Wrap the Corn King tightly in the dried corn husks, like you are enveloping a corpse within a shroud. The entire time you perform these actions, you should project an air of reverence that is usually shown at any other funeral. The Corn King gave his life for a bountiful harvest. It's a bitter-sweet moment. During this ritual, position the Corn King around the Herm until the appropriate time in the ritual comes to consecrate him fully.

(1) Begin the rite by anointing yourself with the oil, using the usual Earth Banishing Pentagram. Pick up the chalice and asperge the area moving in a widdershins pattern, saying any words of cleansing and blessing for the harvest.

(2) Dance widdershins around the pyre to the beat of the drum.

(3) Invoke the presence of the Goddess in her guise as Corn Mother:[38]

> "O UNIVERSAL mother, Ceres fam'd,
> August, the source of wealth, and various nam'd:
> Great nurse, all-bounteous, blessed and divine,
> Who joy'st in peace; to nourish corn is thine.
> Goddess of seed of fruits abundant, fair,
> Harvest and threshing are thy constant care.
> Lovely delightful queen, by all desir'd,
> Who dwell'st in Eleusina's holy vales retir'd.
> Nurse of all mortals, whose benignant mind
> First ploughing oxen to the yoke confin'd;
> And gave to men what nature's wants require,
> With plenteous means of bliss, which all desire.
> In verdure flourishing, in glory bright,
> Assessor of great Bacchus, bearing light:
> Rejoicing in the reapers' sickles, kind,
> Whose nature lucid, earthly, pure, we find.
> Prolific, venerable, nurse divine,

---

[38] To Ceres (XL) from *The Orphic Hymns*, translated by Thomas Taylor, p. 92.

> Thy daughter loving, holy Proserpine.
> A car with dragons yok'd 'tis thine to guide,
> And, orgies singing, round thy throne to ride.
> Only-begotten, much-producing queen,
> All flowers are thine, and fruits of lovely green.
> Bright Goddess, come, with summer's rich
>   increase
> Swelling and pregnant, leading smiling Peace;
> Come with fair Concord and imperial Health,
> And join with these a needful store of wealth."

Pour some Witch's Liquor over the Black Rock and then pour the remainder over the wood on the pyre.

(4) Anoint the Corn King first with oil, then honey, turmeric, beer, and brandy. Any remaining liquids can be tossed onto the pyre as well or saved for your own consumption later on. Say:

> "Come blessed Adonis, various-nam'd,
> Bull-fac'd, begot from thunder, Bacchus fam'd.
> Bassarian God, of universal might,
> Who in swords and blood and sacred rage delight:
> In heaven rejoicing, mad, loud-sounding God,
> Furious inspirer, bearer of the rod:
> By Gods rever'd, who dwell'st with humankind,
> Propitious come, with much rejoicing mind."

(5) Place the Corn King on top of the pyre and light the fire. (6) Toss myrrh into the fire to sweeten the sacrifice.

(7) End the night with revelry. Dance, sing, feast, and make merry! The final thing you should do that night before turning in is brew yourself a strong herbal infusion made from chamomile, spearmint, and passionflower to help with a shamanic journey. Make sure you are not allergic to any of the ingredients of this edible potion. Check with a qualified medical professional if you are unsure, and make any substitutions that are appropriate for your situation. Mix it with honey, a slice of lemon, and a dash of nutmeg. Drink it, thinking about the Corn Wolf and your connection to him in this ritual. It might be a good idea to actually familiarize yourself with the folklore around the Corn

Wolf. Allow yourself to "shapeshift" into the shape of a wolf if you feel called to do so. Run wild and free. Let these themes permeate your subconscious, and, then, when you are done, go immediately to sleep.

Regard the harvest as a personal harvest (and turn the harvest to your advantage), see it as "food for thought." Partake of the lessons that come to you. Garner some wisdom or insight that you didn't have before. Then immediately upon waking, record your experience, and begin the process of composting the "waste" so that it can be used to fertilize next year's cycle.

BIBLIOGRAPHY

Anu, Khepra Ka-Re Amente. *Lifting the Spiritual Self-Esteem of the LGBT Community.* Bloomington, IN: iUniverse Books, 2012.

Bardon, Franz. *Initiation Into Hermetics.* Translated by A. Radspieler. Salt Lake City, UT: Merker Publishing, Inc., 1999.

Baudrillard, Jean. *Seduction.* CTHEORY BOOKS, 2001.

Beckett, John. "Under the Ancient Oaks - I Don't Get Men's Mysteries." *Patheos*, October 18, 2015.

Blount, Ben G., "Issues in Bonobo (Pan paniscus) Sexual Behavior." *American Anthropologist*, vol. 92 (1990).

Bremmer, Jan. "An Enigmatic Indo-European Rite: Paederasty." *Arethusa*, vol. 13, no. 2 (Fall 1980).

Budge, Sir Ernest Alfred Wallis. *The Gods of the Egyptians: Or, Studies in Egyptian Mythology, vol 1.* London, UK: Methuen & Co., 1904.

Burg, B.R. *Sodomy and the Pirate Tradition: English Sea Rovers in the Seventeenth Century Caribbean.* New York: New York University Press, 1984.

Campbell, Joseph. *Historical Atlas of World Mythology.* Vol. 1: *The Way of the Animal Powers,* Part 2, *Mythologies of the Great Hunt.* New York: Harper & Row, 1988.

Canterella, Eva. *Bisexuality in the Ancient World.* Translated by Cormac O'Cuilleanain, New Haven: Yale University Press, 1992.

Carpenter, Edward. *Anthology of Friendship: Iolaus.* London: George Allen & Unwin, 1920.

_____. *Intermediate Types among Primitive Folk, A Study in Social Evolution.* London: George Allen & Co., 1914.

Cartledge, Paul. "The Politics of Spartan Pederasty." *Cambridge Philological Society, Proceedings,* vol. 27 (1981).

Caitlin, George. *Manners, Customs and Condition of the North American Indian.* New York: Dover Publications, 1973.

Chaturvedi, B. K. *Linga Purana.* Vedic Books, 2004.

Chia, Montak & Douglas Abrams. *The Multi-Orgasmic Man.* San Francisco: Harper Collins Publishers, 1997.

Churchill, Wainwright. *Homosexual Behavior among Males: A Cross-Cultural and Cross-Species Investigation.* New York: Hawthorn Books, 1967.

Cicero, Chic and Sandra Tabatha Cicero. *Self-Initiation into the Golden Dawn Tradition.*

Woodbury, MN: Llewellyn Publications, 2012.

Clark, W.M., "Achilles and Patroclus in Love." *Hermes*, vol 106 (1978).

Conner, Randy P. and David Hatfield Sparks. *Cassell's Encyclopedia of Queer Myth, Symbol and Spirit: Gay, Lesbian, Bisexual and Transgendered Lore*. Cassell, 1998.

Crompton, Louis. *Homosexuality and Civilization*. Cambridge, Mass.: Belknap Press of Harvard University Press, 2003.

Daishi, Kobo. *Jitsugokyo: The Wisdom of Kobo Daishi*. Translated by Henry Kawada. CreateSpace Independent Publishing, 2014.

Daniélou, Alain. *Gods of Love and Ecstasy*. Inner Traditions International, Ltd., 1992.

_____. *The Phallus: Sacred Symbol of Male Creative Power*. Rochester, Vermont: Inner Traditions International, 1995.

de Becker, Raymond. *The Other Face of Love*. Translated by Margaret Crosland and Alan Daventry. New York: Grove Press, 1969.

de Laurence, L. W. *The Great Book of Magical Art, Hindu Magic and East Indian Occultism*. Chicago, IL: de Laurence Company, 1915.

Devereaux, George. "Institutionalized Homosexuality of the Mohave Indians." *Human Biology*, vol. 9 (1937).

Dorcey, Peter F. *The Cult of Silvanus: A Study in Roman Folk Religion*. E.J. Brill, 1992.

Dorotez, Raji. *The Scarlet Wand: Sex Magic for Gay Males*. Palermo, CA: Sun Brothers Publishing, 2014.

_____. *The Scarlet Wheel: A Dissertation on the Wheel of the Year and the Eight Sabbats*. Palermo, CA: Sun Brothers Publishing, 2014.

Dover, K.J. *Greek Homosexuality*. New York: Vintage Books, 1980.

_____. "Greek Homosexuality and Initiation." In K.J. Dover, editor, *The Greeks and Their Legacy: Collected Papers. Vol. 2: Prose,*

Literature, History, Society, Transmission, Influence. Oxford and New York: Basil Blackwell, 1988.

Drews, Robert. *The Coming of the Greeks: Indo-European Conquests in the Aegean and the Near East*. Princeton, N.J.: Princeton University Press, 1988.

Duberman, Martin, Martha Vicinus, and George Chauncey, Jr. *Hidden from History: Reclaiming the Gay and Lesbian Past*. New York: Meridian, 1989.

Dumézil, Georges. *Myth to Fiction: the Saga of Hadingus*. Chicago: University of Chicago Press, 1970.

Dynes, Wayne R. *Encyclopedia of Homosexuality*. Edited by Wayne R. Dynes. New York: Garland Publishing Company, 1990.

_____. "Homosexuality in Sub-Saharan Africa: An Unnecessary Question." *Gay Books Bulletin*, vol. 9 (1983).

_____, and Stephen Donaldson, *Ethnographic Studies of Homosexuality*. New York:

Garland Publishing, 1992.

Elledge, Jim. *Masquerade: Queer Poetry in America to the End of World War II*. Bloomington, IN: Indiana University Press, 2004.

Evans, Arthur. *Witchcraft and the Gay Counterculture*. Boston, MA: Fag Rag Books, 1978.

Fortune, Dion. *The Training & Work of an Initiate*. San Francisco, CA: Weiser Books, 2000.

Frazer, Sir James George. *The Golden Bough: A Study in Magic and Religion*, vol. 1, abridged edition. New York: Macmillan Publishing Co., Inc.

Frost, Gavin & Yvonne Frost. *The Solitary Wiccan's Bible: Finding your guides, walking the paths, entering new realms, practicing magic*. ME: Weiser Books, 2004.

_____. *The Witch's Magical Handbook*. Paramus, NJ: Reward Books, 2000.

Furlong, James George Roche. *Faiths of Man: A Cyclopædia of Religions, vol. 2*. Quaritch Publications, Ltd., 1906.

George, Andrew. *The Epic of Gilgamesh: A New Translation*. New York, NY: Penguin Books, 2000.

Gimbutas, Marija. "The Beginning of the Bronze Age in Europe and the Indo-Europeans: 3500-2500 B.C." *Journal of Indo-European Studies*, vol. 1, no. 2 (1973).

Grammaticus, Saxo. *Gesta Denorum: The History of the Danes*. Translated by Peter Fisher. Oxford, UK: Oxford University Press, 2015.

Greenberg, David F. *The Construction of Homosexuality*. Chicago, IL: University of Chicago Press, 1988.

Greeter, Bruce P. *The Secret of the Golden Phallus: Male Erotic Alchemy for the 21st Century*. Maple Shade, NJ: Lethe Press, 2012.

Gwyn. *Light from the Shadows: A Mythos of Modern Traditional Witchcraft*. Capall Bann Publishing, 1999.

Heide, Eldar. "Spinning Siedr." In *Old Norse religion in long-term perspectives*. Edited by Anders Andrén, Kristina Jennbert, and Catharina Raudvere. Lund, Sweden: Nordic Academic Press, 2006.

Heidel, Alexander. *The Gilgamesh Epic and Old Testament Parallels*. Chicago: University of Chicago Press, 1971.

Herdt, Gilbert H. *Guardians of the Flutes*. Chicago: University of Chicago Press, 1981.

Illes, Judika. *Encyclopedia of Spirits, the ultimate guide to the magic of fairies, genies, demons, ghosts, gods & goddesses*. HarperOne, 2009.

_____. *The Element Encyclopedia of Witchcraft*. Harper Element, 2005.

Jackson, Nigel Aldcroft. *Call of the Horned Piper*. Capall Bann Publishing, 1995.

Johnson, Kenneth. *Witchcraft and the Shamanic Journey*. St. Paul, MN: Llewellyn Publications, 1996.

Kaldera, Raven. *Wightridden: Paths of Northern-Tradition Shamanism.* Morrisville, NC: Lulu Enterprises, Inc., 2007.

Kingsley, Peter. *In the Dark Places of Wisdom.* California: Golden Sufi Press, 1999.

Kirsch, John A.W. and James Eric Rodman, "The Natural History of Homosexuality," *Yale Scientific Magazine*, Winter 1977, p.7.

Leek, Sybil. *Diary of a Witch.* Englewood, NJ: The New American Library, 1969.

_____. *The Complete Art of Witchcraft.* New York: Harper & Row, Publishers, Inc., 1971.

Leland, Charles G. *Aradia or the Gospel of the Witches.* The Career Press, Inc., 2003.

Lindemann, Charles. "A Wondrous Tale of a Sperm Tail." *Oakland Journal*, vol 19, Fall 2010.

Mathers, S. Liddell MacGregor (trans). *The Key of Solomon.* San Francisco, CA: Weiser Books, 2000.

Marmor, Judd, editor. *Sexual Inversion: The Multiple Roots of Homosexuality.* New York: Basic Books, 1965.

Macdonell, A. A. *Vedic Mythology.* Oxford, UK: Oxford University Press, 1897.

McKenzie, J. J. *A Gender Neutral God/ess: Be Inclusive but Make No Images was the Religious Change.* United States, 2012.

Mitchell, Stephen. *Gilgamesh.* New York: Atria, 2004.

Mondimore, Francis Mark. *A Natural History of Homosexuality.* Baltimore: Johns Hopkins University Press, 1996.

Morley, Henry. *English Writers: An Attempt Towards a History of English Literature, Vol 1.* Cassel & Company, Limited, 1891.

Nietzsche, Friedrich. *The Birth of Tragedy.* Dover Publications, Inc., 1995.

Neill, James. *The Origins and Role of Same-Sex Relations in Human Society.* McFarland & Company, Inc., 2009.

Paulson, Kathryn. *The Complete Book of Magic & Witchcraft, Revised Edition.* New York: Penguin Group, 1980.

Paxson, Diana L. *Taking Up The Runes.* Red Wheel/Weiser, LLC, 2005.

Penczak, Christopher. *Gay Witchcraft.* San Francisco, CA: Weiser Books, 2003.

Percy, William A. *Pederasty and Pedagogy in Archaic Greece.* Chicago: University of Illinois Press, 1996.

Plato. *Timaeus.* Indianapolis: Hackett Publishing Company, 2001.

Polome, Edgar C. *The Indo-Europeans in the Fourth and Third Millennia.* Ann Arbor: Karoma Publishers, 1982.

Prabhavananda, Swami. "The Concept of Maya." Vedanta Society of Southern California, 26 Sept. 2016.

Pratt, Christina. *An Encyclopedia of Shamanism, Vol 2* (N-Z). The Rosen Publishing Group, Inc., 2007.

Quinn, D. Michael. *Same-Sex Dynamics among Nineteenth-Century Americans.* Chicago, University of Illinois Press, 1996.

Richlin, Amy. *The Garden of Priapus: Sexuality and Aggression in Roman Humor.* New York: Oxford University Press, 1992.

Rowse, A.L. *Homosexuals in History: A Study in Ambivalence in Society, Literature and the Arts.* New York: Carroll & Graf Publishers, 1983.

Saikaku, Ihara. *The Great Mirror of Male Love.* Stanford, CA: Stanford University Press, 1990.

Schmitt, Arno. "Different Approaches to Male-Male Sexuality/Eroticism from Morocco to Usbekistan." In Arno Schmitt and Jehoda Sofer, editors, *Sexuality and Eroticism among Males in Moslem Societies.* New York: Grove Press, 1989.

Schwimmer, Eric. "Male Couples in New Guinea." In Gilbert H. Herdt, *Ritualized Homosexuality in Melanesia.* Los Angeles: University of California Press, 1984.

Stewart, R. J. *Celebrating the Male Mysteries.* Arcania Press, 1992.

Stiles, Mukunda. *Yoga Sutras of Patanjali.* San Francisco, CA: Weiser Books, 2002.

Summers, Claude. *The Queer Encyclopedia of the Visual Arts.* San Francisco, CA: Cleis Press, Inc., 2004.

Tarostar. *The Sacred Pentagraph A Craft Work In Five Volumes.* Left Hand Press, 2015.

Tarrant, Dorothy. "Greek Metaphors of Light," *The Classical Quarterly, Vol 10, No. 2*, pp. 181-187. Cambridge University Press, 1960.

Vanggaard, Thorkill. *Phallos: A Symbol and Its History in the Male World.* New York: International Universities Press, 1972.

Williams, Walter L. *The Spirit and the Flesh: Sexual Diversity in American Indian Culture.* Boston, MA: Beacon Press, 1992.

GETTING IN TOUCH

I would love to hear back from you about your experiences with this book and its rituals. I believe that rediscovery the Male Mysteries must be a collective effort, and I'm excited to participate in that effort with each of you. If you would like to talk with me directly, you can reach me through my website at either:

www.caseygiovinco.com
www.facebook.com/hexebeast/

If you are interested in exploring the Male Mysteries with other Gay and Bisexual Pagan Men, you can join one of the many Facebook groups that Gala Witchcraft maintains as a community service to the general Pagan Public at:

https://www.facebook.com/groups/gaymalewitches/

We also maintain a group for Straight, Bisexual, Gay, as well as Transgender Men at:

https://www.facebook.com/groups/malepaganmysteries/

And, finally, we maintain a group on the Male Mysteries open to anyone who's interested (male, female, Transgender, gay, straight, bisexual, asexual). If you're interested in talking about this book or the Male Mysteries, in general, it's a great group with a very diverse group of members. You can get in touch there at:

https://www.facebook.com/groups/wiccagarbedingreen/

Finally, if you loved what you read here and you would like to join one the covens within Gala Witchcraft, you can reach out to us at one of the links below:

www.galawitchcraft.com
https://www.facebook.com/groups/covenmellona/

Thank you again for reading this book. I look forward to meeting you. Blessed Be, Casey Giovinco.

ABOUT THE AUTHOR

Casey Giovinco is Chief Elder of Gala Witchcraft, which combines traditional coven-based, initiatory Wicca with the central goal of reawakening the Gay Mysteries. In addition to his work with Gala, Casey works with clients in a variety of modalities, applying the metaphysical principles he learned through his Wiccan clergy training to improve the quality of their lives. He is an RYT 200 yoga teacher, and he holds certifications in strategic organizational leadership from Villanova University, hypnosis from the National Guild of Hypnotists, and life, executive, and relationship coaching from The Coach Training Alliance.